The CUSTOMER Journey

HOW AN OWNED AUDIENCE CAN TRANSFORM YOUR BUSINESS

Written by

Mike Huber

Brad Kuenn

Shana Sullivan

Blake Pappas

Drew Eastmead

Design & Illustration by

Kate Gearin

The CUSTOMER Journey

Connect
with the Authors

Mike Huber

🐦 @mjhuber
in linkedin.com/in/mikehuber
@ MikeH@verticalmeasures.com

Brad Kuenn

🐦 @BKuenn22
in www.linkedin.com/in/brad-kuenn
@ BradK@verticalmeasures.com

Shana Sullivan

🐦 @ShanaSullivan38
in linkedin.com/in/shanasullivan1
@ ShanaS@verticalmeasures.com

Drew Eastmead

🐦 @dreweastmead
in linkedin.com/in/dreweastmead
@ Drew@tensiondesign.com

Blake Pappas

🐦 @blakepappas22
in linkedin.com/in/blake-pappas
@ BlakeP@verticalmeasures.com

Connect
with the Designer

Kate Gearin

@irish.kate

KateG@verticalmeasures.com

Legal Mumbo-jumbo

Fist Bumps
for Our Book

"Thoughtful and complete perspective from marketing experts sharing their hard-won experience. Get, and read it cover to cover, before your competitors do!"

- Tim Ash, CEO of SiteTuners, international marketing keynote speaker, bestselling author

"Hugely useful guide to consumer decision-making and how to win awareness and drive behavior at every stage. Practical and modern; highly recommended!"

- Jay Baer, founder of Convince & Convert and author of Talk Triggers

"Cutting through the noise, Vertical Measures continues to drive innovation on the front lines of digital marketing. As told through Sophia's story, the Vertical Measures team speaks the truth learned from many years spent improving their effectiveness and helping clients become more successful. Through thoughtfulness and hard work, they've developed the winning formula."

- Joe Bockerstette, Partner at Business Enterprise Mapping

"We've been moving away from brand-centric to customer-focused marketing for some time. While most marketers understand the need to engage audiences and build trust, we need examples and stories to support our cause. That's where The Customer Journey comes in. Not only does it solve the problem most marketers are facing when trying to demonstrate results from customer-focused marketing, but it does so using the compelling story of Sophia's own customer journey. This is a must-read for digital marketers."

- Michael Brenner, Author, Speaker, Consultant and CMO

"It's too easy for marketers to get caught up in the mechanics of their craft and forget the fundamentals of the customer experience and journey. I love how the Customer Journey covers the layers of details without losing sight of why we're doing all this. Highly recommended!"

- Doug Bruhnke, CEO/founder of Global Chamber®

"The Customer Journey has cracked the code on vividly explaining the modern buying process. Every business needs to deeply understand how their buyers think at every stage of their buying process and craft the right experiences for each stage. This book will help you put yourselves in your customers' shoes from the outside in."

- Greg Head, CEO, Scaling Point

"Teaching customer journey mapping by mapping a customer journey through the compelling story of Sophia, including real-world examples. How meta — and brilliant — of you all at Vertical Measures. Bravo for turning your data into drama to help us experience and apply the wisdom in these pages."

- Park Howell, Storytelling Keynote Speaker,
Host of Business of Story Podcast

"The biggest change in marketing over the last decade isn't marketing at all — the biggest change is the way people buy. Demand creation for products and services has given way to guiding the customer journey or something more akin to organizing buying behavior. Seem complicated? The Customer Journey will teach you everything you need to know."

- John Jantsch, Author of Duct Tape Marketing and
The Referral Engine

"What are consumers doing? How are consumers doing it? Consumers are on a journey. Is your brand a grand part of the adventure or a traffic jam/unwanted detour? Here's the answer. Read it. Do it. Be the consumer's co-pilot."

- Mitch Joel, Six Pixels of Separation & CTRL ALT Delete.

"Our world is now full of self-educated customers on a quest for answers that solve their biggest problems. Will you be the one to deliver them?"

- Carla Johnson, Keynote speaker,
best-selling author and storyteller

"The Customer Journey provides a clear, pragmatic approach to developing an organizational content strategy that suits your consumers needs along the entire purchase journey. This book is the most important strategic-SEO read of the year."

- Ken Kralick, Head of Global Ecommerce, PUMA SE

"Truly amazing insights from a world-class team! Absolutely brilliant. Congrats guys — it's a homerun!"

- Mike Roberts, Founder of SpyFu and Nacho Analytics

"When we talk about modern marketing, apostrophes matter. It is the customer's journey. Customer is not just an adjective, and the journey is certainly not yours. This book is a wonderful guide, and timely reminder, that our content and marketing efforts need to be squarely focused on exactly what our audience needs to hear, not what we need to say."

- Robert Rose, Chief Strategy Officer,
The Content Advisory

"Well written and takes a unique perspective on the issues we all face on how to attract more customers in this digital market. Not just a book of 'how-to' but an understanding of 'why'...thank you for sharing!"

- Paul Zagnoni, President, Brighton College

"Blending the contemporary practices of developing deep customer experience insights with how to optimize brand and marketing communications for each step of the customer journey, this book delivers for anyone seeking to map their investments in marketing directly to every aspect of the customer journey. The outcome? A profitable and sustainable relationship between one's brand and customers. Perhaps most impressive, this book is a story about Sophia's search for higher education. A story just like the ones brands must tell to connect with customers."

- Jeff Walters, Partner at True North Companies, co-Founder
ClickSquared & Targetbase

Table **of Contents**

Acknowledgments

Anyone who has ever written a book knows how hard it is to write the first one, let alone the second one. This is Vertical Measures' third. Admittedly, our team knew we needed to write an updated resource that would help guide fellow marketers over the next few years. But, like many content-creators, we felt the overwhelming weight of a project this size. So, procrastinate we did. It wasn't until Mike Huber, a man of many ideas and aspirations, came to Arnie Kuenn with a fresh concept based off a presentation **Jonah Deaver** created for a higher-education workshop.

Instead of placing the burden of writing a new book on a single person, we'd write it as a team. Afterall, our culture is all about being **#InItTogether**, and we knew that if we put our heads together, we could create something truly special. Developing something like this requires a dedicated team, and for us, it consisted of the following people (we sure hope we haven't forgotten anyone):

The creative behind this project is all thanks to **Kate Gearin**. The cover and every graphic in this book were designed by her. She dealt with our excitement, concerns, impatience, naivety and ever-changing deadlines with patience and professionalism. When we had dumb ideas she told us, when we had too many ideas she tackled them, when she had great ideas she let us take all the credit.

Diane Porter, an experienced writer and editor, has worked with Vertical Measures for several years. She agreed to jump in and serve as our dedicated editor on this book. Her expertise was invaluable, especially when navigating different writing styles and tones from our co-authors. If you are contemplating writing a book, you might want Diane on your team.

Denielle Kelley acted as the project manager, making sure everyone stayed on track (for the most part). This book, quite literally, could not have happened without her.

At Vertical Measures, it didn't stop there. **Erik Solan**, our VP of Client Services & Strategy, **Jim Bader**, our Senior Director of SEO, and **Lianna Kissinger Virizlay**, our Senior Director of Content, served as subject matter experts, making sure we were accurate when it came to the paid advertising, SEO and content topics. **Arnie Kuenn** was gracious enough to write the foreword. The entire VM team helped.

Most importantly, we would like to thank our families. We could not have done this without your constant love and support. Thank you.

- Brad, Mike, Shana, Blake & Drew

Dedicated to Wendy Huber

Foreword
By Arnie Kuenn

Why should every marketing executive read this book?

As the founder and CEO of Vertical Measures, I've led the team that wrote this book for a few years now. Having written one of the first content marketing books to hit the market (*Accelerate!*) in 2011, and co-authoring the follow-up book, *Content Marketing Works*, in 2015, I know firsthand the time and effort it took for this team to create this incredibly helpful book. Their dedication to the topic and the task of creating it was awe-inspiring.

Though the book is written by the team at Vertical Measures, you will quickly realize it is not about our agency or our services. It is a beautifully crafted story about Sophia pursuing her online MBA, with a marketing concentration, at Coronado University. It's about the journey she takes to decide what her marketing career path looks like, the degree she wants to pursue, and which school she will attend to obtain that degree. In other words, her customer journey.

I am honored that the authors asked me to write the foreword. They could have asked anyone (honest), but they felt my experience in teaching tens of thousands of digital marketing students around the world, and my previous writing experience, would be valuable to you — the reader.

What makes this book different? Why should you take the time to read it? How will it help you grow your business?

Based on my real-world experiences, I'm willing to bet that you are at a crossroads with your digital marketing. Whether you are the CMO, the CEO or the marketing manager, my bet is you totally understand the digital marketing landscape, you were one of the early adopters, you are already ahead of many of your competitors, and you have some staff in place to help you accomplish your company's goals.

BUT… it isn't quite clicking (pun intended) the way you had hoped and the way the pundits said it should happen. I am also willing to bet you are not following a documented digital marketing strategy and are not focused on building your owned audience.

This book is the perfect blend of solid "how-to" information and a story that is relatable and easy to follow. It's geared toward you marketing leaders and focuses on helping you become more successful with the same – or less effort – than you are currently investing.

It will show you:

- How to create and use a documented strategy.
- How to truly understand your customers' journeys.
- How to build your owned audience.
- How some subtle changes to tactics you probably employ today will drastically increase your level of success in growing your organization's revenue.

This book is a joint effort of five subject-matter experts, and it shows. The authors bring their vast knowledge and experience to light with easy-to-read charts, specific examples, and tools you can use, all while maintaining the central story: Sophia's customer journey.

However, the devil is in the details. As with any course you take, workshop you attend, or book you read, there is a lot of information being presented and consumed. This book is no different. The details really do matter. When the authors present what should be included in a strategy, how to brainstorm and create the right content, how to create a culture of content, how to optimize and promote that content, how to implement lead nurture, why building your own audience is so important, and most importantly, why the executives at your company need to lead the way, they mean it.

The book is based on these authors teaching and interacting with thousands of marketers every year. They truly know why one organization succeeds and another organization fails when it comes to marketing. We have literally lived this book.

It took the team 18 months from concept to publishing, but it's been 13 years in the making. I highly recommend it to all of you interested in growing your business online in this and the next decade.

Read on!

Arnie Kuenn

Founder and CEO, Vertical Measures
VerticalMeasures.com

Introduction
What will be different about this book?

It's been four years since Arnie Kuenn (and the team at Vertical Measures) published *Content Marketing Works: 8 Steps To Transform Your Business*. The initial concept was to provide a step-by-step "how-to" book on content marketing. We knew our audience needed a resource on how to use content to market their businesses, and *Content Marketing Works* would be that answer for them. Although we've shifted focus to the Customer Journey and Building Your Owned Audience, we still use the 8 steps, and find them extremely effective for not only our company, but our clients as well. As quickly as the content marketing landscape changes, we're proud that *Content Marketing Works* still holds strong as a go-to resource, offering a valuable blueprint for marketers who are just starting to build their strategies, or looking for ways to convince their bosses to go "all in" on content marketing.

Back then, Arnie would teach workshops around the country and start by asking his audience a simple question: "How many of you have heard of, or know what content marketing is?" Less than 50 percent of the crowd would comfortably raise their hands.

Today, it's a different story. We have more team members traveling around the country to speak, and more of our audience understands the basics of content marketing and the true value of it. We may get a lot of people to raise their hands for that question now, but when we follow it up with, "How many of you have been successful at content marketing for 12 months in a row?" the hands drop back down.

Four years is a long time in this industry. A lot can happen. It's clear that although many marketers get the general concepts of content marketing, they're still trying to figure out how to fine-tune their strategies to generate the biggest ROI for their businesses. And that isn't for a lack of effort.

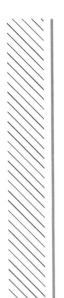

Just think about some of the trends we've witnessed come and go since *Content Marketing Works* was published:

- Google Glass was an epic fail
- Google+ missed the mark
- Vine was trimmed by Twitter
- Digg was overpowered by Reddit's community

But, there were also some clear winners:

- Marketing strategies for mobile-first continue to evolve
- Influencer marketing has shown clear value
- Paid media promotion is booming
- Link building still hasn't died (it's just changed)
- Demand for video and interactive content is at an all-time high

Want to know what hasn't changed in four years? People still spend an enormous amount of their time online. MultiView, a B2B digital marketing provider, pulled together some statistics on how your potential customers apply their time online.[1] Led by CEO Scott Bedford, the agency noted that most users spend a whopping 7 to 8 hours online throughout the day. This can involve a lot of different types of online activity, from checking email at work to commenting on a friend's most recent poolside selfie. Luckily for marketers, you can reach the majority of these potential customers online, regardless of where they are or what they're doing on the web.

Engaging on social media

Users spend more than 28 percent of their time online using social media to engage with friends, family and businesses. Keep in mind that today, more than 80 percent of this activity occurs on a mobile device.

Marketing opportunity

Use digital display ads on social media networks like Facebook, Twitter and LinkedIn for your audience as they browse their feeds and engage with brands.

---

1 https://www.multiview.com/resources/infographics/time-online-breakdown/

Checking email

About 24 percent of the average user's time online is spent checking and sending emails.

Marketing opportunity

Believe it or not, inboxes get more engagement than any other marketing channel. Lead nurturing emails and newsletters are fantastic opportunities to build a trusting relationship with your audience.

Reading content

Around 23 percent of a user's time online is spent reading blog posts, interactive content, eBooks and industry reports.

Marketing opportunity

Target your specific audience segments on websites they frequent most often with high-quality content that leads them down the sales funnel.

Watching videos

The typical user spends close to 19 percent of their time online watching video each day.

Marketing opportunity

Video marketing is on the rise. It offers brands ways to reach audiences not just in advertisements, but also video overlay ads and display ads surrounding the player and more.

Shopping

Roughly 6 percent of time online is spent shopping for new products or services. These activities can include shopping for something small like new shoes or for a big purchase like an in-ground pool.

Marketing opportunity

Consistently post relevant content to stay top-of-mind with your audience and use efficient calls-to-action to optimize your conversion rates.

Researching information

Only 1 percent of an average user's day is spent searching for information on search engines like Google, Bing and Yahoo.

Marketing opportunity

Although this amount of time seems short, it shows that much of the time spent online happens after the initial research. You might be able to ideate and create awesome content that shows up on Page 1 of the search engine results page (SERP), but if you don't nurture that traffic and continue to build a relationship, you'll miss out on a lot of potential business.

How People Spend Their Time Online

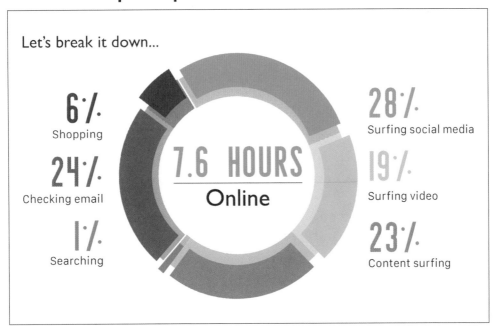

Let's break it down...

6% Shopping

24% Checking email

1% Searching

7.6 HOURS Online

28% Surfing social media

19% Surfing video

23% Content surfing

Figure #1: How potential customers apply their time online (Source: MultiView)

Reaching out to customers while they're using the Internet means that you must engage them in what they're doing online. From the list above, it's evident that the critical mass for your digital marketing strategy will center on the top three reasons people are online: to learn, to have fun, and to socialize.

The smaller part of the strategy (arguably more important), is to nurture those relationships and move a prospect down the sales funnel toward becoming a loyal customer.

You may want them to shop on your site, for example, but you connect with them by providing some form of useful content that leads them to your site. Users want to engage with the content they find. That is, they want to stay on the page and interact with it or learn from it. If the content doesn't engage them, solve a problem, or answer a question — they move on (or bounce) and continue searching.

 "49% of digital media consumption is through a mobile device."

-MultiView

Remember,
search engines still have the same goal

The mission of any search engine — particularly Google, the giant in this arena — is to find the best and most relevant content for a person's search term.

Here's Google's stated philosophy:

"The perfect search engine would understand exactly what you mean and give you back exactly what you want."

This is a pretty high bar, but it's what every search engine tries to do because that's what users demand. The competition among search engines is driven by the results they can bring back.

Knowing that search engines are going to generate results that closely match a searcher's inquiry, and sometimes, intent, it's up to you as a publisher (yes, you are a publisher) to get content in front of them at the right time.

And for this reason, Vertical Measures is taking another stab at predicting a digital marketing trend: strategizing around the customer journey while building your owned audience — one you can reach at the time and place of your choosing.

What's changed is the customer journey

The customer journey is the process your audience goes through to purchase a new product or service. While different marketers have their own detailed versions of the customer journey, Vertical Measures considers four key benchmarks:

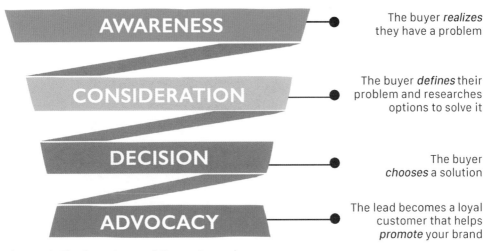

AWARENESS	The buyer *realizes* they have a problem
CONSIDERATION	The buyer *defines* their problem and researches options to solve it
DECISION	The buyer *chooses* a solution
ADVOCACY	The lead becomes a loyal customer that helps *promote* your brand

Figure #2: The four stages of the customer journey

How do you define your customer's journey?

If you don't have an intimate understanding of your audience and prospects, it can be extremely difficult to accurately define your unique customer's journey.

"68% of B2B organizations haven't even defined the stages in their sales funnels."

- MarketingSherpa

Consider the following questions as you put together the customer's journey for your company:

During the Awareness stage, your audience can meet you for the first time through both traditional and digital promotion.

For the Awareness stage, ask yourself:

- How do you start the conversation before the customer knows there's a need?
- What are my customers asking about their needs or challenges?
- How are my customers educating themselves about these challenges?
- How can I provide resources for my customers that address their needs?
- How do I provide an answer while building a trusted relationship with them?
- How do I spark enough interest in my product/service to move them to the next stage?

During the Consideration stage, your customers will most likely have a clearly defined goal or challenge. They're currently researching and evaluating their options before making a buying decision.

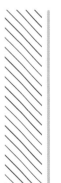

For the Consideration stage, ask yourself:

- What types of solutions are my customers evaluating and where does my company fit in?
- What types of content are my customers consuming as they evaluate their options?
- How are my customers perceiving the pros and cons of each solution to their challenges?
- How do my customers decide which solution is right for them?

During the Decision stage, your customers have evaluated their options and identified your products or services as a viable option to solve their challenges. They're deciding on which product or service to purchase, and will soon convert to a paying customer.

For the Decision stage, ask yourself:

- What qualifiers did my customers use to evaluate their options?
- When customers researched their options, what did they like about my company compared to alternatives?
- What concerns do they still have with my products or services?
- What are my customer's expectations?

During the Advocacy stage, you've successfully gained a new customer by directing them through the sales funnel, and becoming a trusted partner. Now it's time to nurture them to become repeat or long-term customers who advocate for your brand. These loyal customers will entice others to use your products or services based on their own success.

For the Advocacy stage, ask yourself:

- Who is this advocate and how does their journey relate to my current audience?
- How can this new advocate help influence others to consider my products or services?
- What questions can the advocate answer for my audience?
- How can I promote their testimonial to reach a wide audience?

The answers to these questions will provide a greater understanding of each stage of the customer journey. Use each benchmark to ultimately reach the same goal: Lead your audience through the sales funnel, until they eventually become loyal customers and advocates for your brand. Your website and the content you present has the power to lead them through their journey.

Some journeys are fast, some are slow

It's important to remember that depending on your industry or mapped customer journey, the time it takes to get your audience from the awareness stage to the advocacy stage may vary. In fact, each journey may be different depending on what type of content you have available and how it's promoted (whether digitally or traditionally).

Let's look at two quick examples of a customer journey from a B2B and B2C perspective:

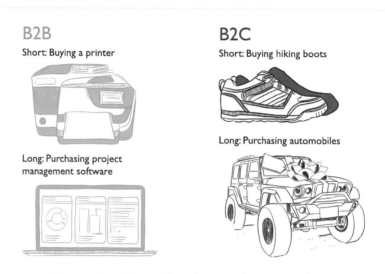

B2B
Short: Buying a printer

Long: Purchasing project management software

B2C
Short: Buying hiking boots

Long: Purchasing automobiles

Figure #3: Short vs. long customer journey examples (B2B & B2C)

For this reason, it's vital for you to try and understand your own customer's journey. The importance of establishing a digital marketing strategy (and backing it up with measurement at each stage of the journey) cannot be overstated.

Look, you cannot improve, change, or build your customer journey without measuring the successes and failures. You need to measure how your content is performing at every stage, and adopt the mindset that measurement is absolutely critical to the success of your company.

Throughout this book, it's your job to consider your own customer's journey. While every company is different, you'll be amazed at the similar habits of people shopping for a product or service online. Although our book focuses on a single B2C customer journey, your company can see the same success from a B2B perspective, as long as the customer journey is properly mapped out.

It's not how, it's why

Our fist two books, *Accelerate!* and *Content Marketing Works,* were both bonafide "how-to" books that assisted marketers just beginning to discover the world of content marketing. Our goal for this book, however, is to explain why companies map out their customer's journey to lead them down the sales funnel.

ROI is important — business owners would argue that it's the central aspect of investing in digital marketing. In fact, when asked what metrics were viewed as most important when investing in marketing, more than 80 percent of CEOs (B2B and B2C) said better conversion rates and sales were critical toward their making their decisions.

Most Important Metrics
B2B Content Marketers Use

Metric	Value
Sales Lead Quality	87%
Sales	84%
Higher Conversion Rates	82%
Sales Lead Quantity	71%
Website Traffic	71%
Brand Lift	69%
SEO Ranking	67%
Customer Renewal Rates	66%
Purchase Intent	64%
Subscriber Growth	62%

Figure #4a: Most important B2B metrics (Source: 2017 CMI B2B Trends Report)

Most Important Metrics B2C Content Marketers Use

Metric	Percent
Sales	85%
Higher Conversion Rates	80%
Website Traffic	79%
Sales Lead Quality	78%
SEO Ranking	75%
Sales Lead Quantity	73%
Customer Renewal Rates	72%
Brand Lift	71%
Social Media Sharing	67%
Purchase Intent	66%

Figure #4b: Most important B2C metrics (Source: 2018 CMI B2C Trends Report)

"Content Marketing ROI is no harder than ROI for the rest of marketing. But many folks ask the question more as a defense mechanism for change. You will hear marketers ask this question despite not knowing what the ROI is on the rest of their marketing spend. So, start with that benchmark. What is the ROI of marketing? Content marketing ROI is easier because content marketing results are easier than something like advertising."

- Michael Brenner, CEO Marketing Insider Group

In order to generate the type of ROI that would deem digital marketing a success, you need to not only understand *how* to use content, SEO and paid media to market your brand, but also *why* you use them to market your brand.

We've already written two "step-by-step" books on how to generate the biggest return on your content marketing investment. Now, to provide a better understanding of digital marketing best practices as a whole, we're going to explain why your customers interact the way they do online.

We're going to explain why they perform searches at different stages, why brands target them the way they do, and why you need to reach your audience at each and every benchmark of the customer's journey.

In other words: You understand *how* it happens, now let's dive deeper and begin to understand *why* it all happens.

Why we chose an MBA as our example

We know a little bit about you. You may have spent thousands of dollars to hear people like us speak for 45 minutes at conferences about what it means to create that awesome content. We put up 20 or 30 slides and tell you what you should be doing and get you psyched about the possibilities. You understand the general concept of digital marketing, and see a clear value in using content to generate more traffic, leads, and sales for your business.

But there's been a growing shift around digital marketing — most industries know what it is, but few are doing it correctly. You've watched the webinars, bookmarked a few resources online, and tried your hand at a digital marketing strategy. After a few rounds of publishing content, you noticed a boost in traffic and felt excited: "Holy crap, this is actually working!" Fast forward a month or two, you're still following the same best practices we've been cramming down your throat, but you're not generating the same type of traffic, engagement, or leads from that first month of excitement.

You're most likely experiencing the emotional journey of digital marketing, or nearing what's known as the "Trough of Disillusionment." It looks something like this:

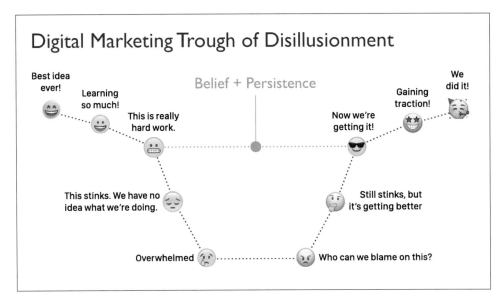

Figure #5: Digital Marketing Trough of Disillusionment

Our team learned about this path not only by experiencing it ourselves, but also by hearing about it from our own clients. Most of our audience is made up of fellow marketers, and you've probably experienced something like the Trough of Disillusionment. You've followed the best practices, published a lot of amazing content for your own audience, and aren't seeing the results you were expecting.

 **You scream out, "WHY?! I've done everything right! I've strategized, brainstormed, created content, published, promoted, distributed! What am I missing?"**

When the Vertical Measures team came up with the concept for our new book, we knew we wanted to tell a single story that's easily relatable, and that would allow our readers (marketers) to put themselves in the shoes of our protagonist and example companies. No more jumbled timelines or puzzles to put together. We're telling one story — from start to finish — about a marketer looking to go back to school and advance her career to become Chief Marketing Officer (CMO) of a marketing agency. We will follow her from beginning to end as she researches her education options and eventually has two universities competing for her enrollment.

Spoiler Alert:

Only one university is utilizing the customer journey correctly. Will you relate more with the university that's succeeding, or the one that's failing?

Eliminating content gaps

In our story, you'll follow our protagonist as she searches for the university that's best for her, and even watch her drop off from a competitor's sales funnel due to a large content gap in their customer journey. We wanted to illustrate, in real time, what it's like for a consumer to experience a content gap along their journey to becoming a loyal customer. Your business cannot afford to have these content gaps. If you do, potential customers will have no choice but to leave your company behind and find solutions to their challenges elsewhere.

So, let's assume you've started your own digital marketing strategy. You've got plenty of traffic to the website, you've got a few leads coming in, but you can't seem to close the sale. This is a common struggle for businesses and their sales teams.

What's happening? Most likely, there's a misalignment between your available content and the customer journey. Properly mapping content to your customers directly affects the success of any digital marketing campaign.

"65% of marketers are still challenged when it comes to understanding which types of content are effective and which types aren't."

-TopRank Blog

John Bertino, founder of The Agency Guy Inc., believes content gaps are easily identified by search engines: "Google and other search engines want nothing more than to serve up results that fully and completely answer user search queries. There is arguably no better way for marketers to achieve this than by being crystal clear about what our various audience personas are thinking about and asking about during each stage of the buyer's journey. Effectively answering those queries by getting the right content in front of the right persona at the right time is essentially the holy grail of SEO."

Answer questions people are *actively searching* for in Google

It doesn't matter how cool you think your products or services are, or what you believe people should read about... if your audience isn't actively searching for that type of content, you're already creating content gaps in the customer's journey. Most of the time, successful content has nothing to do with your writing skills, or how many long-tail keyword phrases you can stuff into the copy. Great content depends on thoughtful ideation (brainstorming) and actually answering your audience's most common questions.

As disappointing as it may sound, search engines are not going to recognize your fancy words or rank your content higher because it showcases groundbreaking products that are sold on your website. Instead, search engines are designed to match up results based on relevancy, which makes creating content around what people are actively searching for vitally important. What we see, more often than not, is content efforts failing because people are simply not searching for what you've created.

So, the (common) question is: How do you create content people are actually searching for?

The sales person in all of us wants to focus immediately on getting prospects to shop on your website. We get it. It's difficult to sacrifice time and effort to create content that doesn't directly sell your product or service. However, by only publishing the "close-the-deal" type content, you can actually hurt your chances of converting visitors because they simply aren't ready to make a buying decision.

Remember the numbers we listed previously: only 6 percent of the time spent online is used for making buying decisions. There is a lot more research, engagement and nurturing that takes place before reaching that lower funnel content. Consider this guideline:

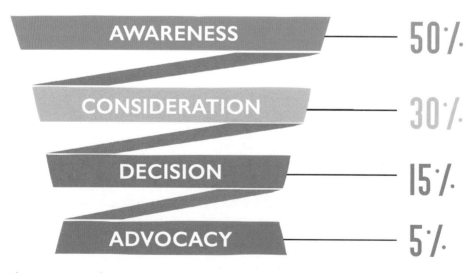

Figure #6: Nurturing content rule by Vertical Measures

This rule separates top, middle and lower funnel content so that you can be sure most of the content you're publishing casts the largest net — reaching the most people. As you continue building relationships with your visitors, your focus (and the content) will narrow to that lower-funnel content.

How do you know what type of content to create? Let's refresh your memory on some ideation basics:

One of the easiest ways to generate awesome content ideas is by utilizing the wealth of knowledge already at your fingertips — your employees.

For example:

Ask your staff or sales representatives what questions they get asked every day. Feel free to include anyone who talks to current or prospective clients.

Look through company studies, surveys and reports that might help identify what your customers are most concerned with.

If you actively participate in trade shows, talk with those who worked your booth to see what topics were most prominent in their conversations.

These three examples are great ways to identify content ideas for all top-, middle- and bottom-funnel topics. Regardless of where your audience is in their journey, focus on creating content that offers solutions to their queries, whether that be in search engines, answers sites, or other forums. If you're currently creating content for your blog, there might be a plethora of good questions in the comments section of existing content. Use these questions to form follow-up posts or fresh content.

These ideas will naturally create a "content blanket" that covers different stages of your customer's journey and provides a valuable resource for your audience. If you're a little behind, don't worry, we'll cover effective ideation in Chapter 3.

When creating content, be the best answer on the internet.

- Andy Crestodina,
Cofounder Orbit Media Studios

As we've been saying for years, "If you have a website, you're a publisher, and you have to think like one." This means producing fresh content on a regular basis. Print publishers create content to survive, because that's their business. On the internet, it's the same for you. You need to keep thinking about content ideas all the time. You should encourage your entire staff to do the same. Because as you will learn during our story, if you have a content gap in your customer journey, you'll miss golden opportunities to generate more revenue.

Hopefully by now, you've adopted a content marketing mindset and are always on the lookout for new content possibilities. Keep a little notebook on hand or create a note on your phone so that when you get a great idea for a top-10 list, you can record the idea. When you attend an event, take pictures and videos so you can post images of the event on your blog or social channels.

You can't create something cool once and let it sit idly online, expecting it to be cutting edge or consistently relevant to users. Instead, your job is to keep producing fresh material, even repurposing your best content, so that it reappears in a fresh form and gives you as many different opportunities to be found during the customer's journey.

In order to help move your audience through their journey and become a loyal customer to your brand, prepare for some serious effort. For any marketing person, mapping out a complete customer's journey can require a major commitment of time and energy. We've found that many businesses don't have the budget to add more bodies to their staff to tackle the objectives in a content marketing program, so they have to juggle existing resources.

How can organizations make it work?

Top down buy-in is still critical, especially for small businesses. Key executives in your organization need to recognize that a content marketing strategy is crucial to their success on the internet, and they need to understand that they, too, will have to participate. Once the top has bought-in, you can get the rest of the staff involved. There's a place for everyone to help create content and reach your audience at each stage of the journey.

Above all, top-down buy-in means that you can look to anyone and everyone to provide inspiration and new ideas to reach your audience. Foster a fun environment where creative expression is valued. The more you encourage creativity, the more you can gain from your content marketing strategy. And always remember, just because you wrote it, took a picture of it or shot a video, it doesn't mean you have to publish it. But you must start creating content with the intent of using it. Your content will do nothing if it sits on your desktop.

Without further ado

We're excited to take you on this journey, from frustration to success with digital marketing. We're confident that by the end of this book, you'll have an expert understanding of the customer's journey and why applying these principles to your evolving digital marketing strategy is the key to success.

Let's begin our journey and meet our protagonist, Sophia...

CHAPTER I
Meet Sophia

Our protagonist in this story is Sophia West, a first-generation American living in beautiful San Diego, California.

Sophia's parents are both immigrants — her mom moved to the U.S. from Mexico City at age 23; her father migrated from Sicily, Italy, when he was just 19. Her father loves telling stories about growing up in the town of Villafranca di Verona, stomping on grapes as a child to earn money for the family, avoiding Mafiosos in the '60s and immigrating to the United States with only 30 cents in his pocket.

Sophia's parents built a successful life for themselves, from very humble beginnings, through hard work and dedication to their craft. They instilled these life principles, always pushing education and working hard. After growing up in a home filled with loving, hardworking role models, she understands the effort it takes to reach professional and personal goals. Sophia is married to a supportive husband; they have two young children together, and a dog named Sugar.

Sophia is a marketing professional with five years of experience at an agency named Stonecreek Digital.

Because of the high cost of living in San Diego and motivation to provide for her family, she's inspired to earn more money and advance her career.

"Cost continues to be the biggest reservation for prospective students, with many concerned that business school may require more money than they have available (51%) or they may need to take on large debts (46%)."

- Graduate Management Admission Council (GMAC)

Not only is the cost of living high in San Diego, Sophia (like many of us) has debt from student loans. She completed her Bachelor of Science degree in marketing back in 2014 and enjoys her role as brand marketing specialist for Stonecreek Digital, but Sophia wants more than a higher salary.

While there are opportunities to grow within Stonecreek Digital, Sophia is motivated to take on a leadership role and high-level position at a mid- to large-size company or with a larger marketing agency. She's known as a critical thinker, is looked up to by her peers in the office and wears many hats, from brainstorming ideas for creative content to collaborating with clients and coworkers and measuring success. While this role provides her with a chance to get creative and work directly with clients, Sophia has limited opportunity to influence their marketing campaigns. Sophia never settles. She wants more.

This book follows Sophia's journey as she becomes aware of her options in advanced degrees, considers her degree and school options, decides which degree to pursue at which university, and advocates for the program she ultimately chooses.

She stays up-to-date
on marketing trends

Sophia spends close to four hours each day reading blog posts, industry reports and thought-leadership pieces (just don't tell her boss that). She follows several marketing experts, or influencers, on LinkedIn and has built a small community on the network. These influencers regularly publish content that Sophia follows, reads, and shares.

Figure #7: Robert Rose's LinkedIn profile (Source: LinkedIn)

Figure #8: David Meerman Scott's LinkedIn profile (Source: LinkedIn)

Carla Johnson • 1st
Global Keynote Speaker, Best-Selling
Author, Storyteller

Parker, Colorado

Connect   More...

Carla Johnson Keynote
Speaker and Best-
Selling Author

Cooper Professional
Education

See contact info

500+ connections

Figure #9: Carla Johnson's LinkedIn profile (Source: LinkedIn)

Stephen Reilly • 1st
Marketing Guru, Micro-influencer,
Storyteller

Nova Scotia, Canada

Connect   More...

MBA, Marketing Guru

Magellan University

See contact info

500+ connections

Figure #10: Stephen Reilly's LinkedIn profile

She uses these connections to advance her professional aspirations

Building these connections is all part of reaching Sophia's professional goals. Her inspiration for getting a marketing degree was to lead a creative team of marketers and climb the corporate ladder toward the C suite. It's become clear during her time at Stonecreek Digital that if she wants to lead her own team and earn a bigger salary, she needs an advanced degree in business, marketing or a related field. In Sophia's mind, however, her busy schedule with kids, family, work, and daily activities makes going back to school a far-off dream.

"Prospective students are very deliberate about their postgraduate career path. 71% of prospects cite a single industry of interest for postgraduate employment."

– Graduate Management Admission Council (GMAC)

Sophia wonders what career path is right for her. During her drive home, Sophia often reflects on a hard day's work; she wonders what's next for her career and personal life. Her thoughts are filled with both optimism and frustration. She's excited to keep working toward a brighter future, but feels anxious that things aren't moving fast enough. She's thinking through what's next but unaware of the options to go back to school and make those dreams a reality.

Her online habits are just like yours

Sophia spends more than 70 percent of her time online surfing content, watching videos and engaging on her social media networks. Most of her activity is work-related, but some of it is silly click-bait to pass time during lunch. Only 1 percent of her time online is spent conducting searches in Google.[2] This might seem like a small percentage, but it's absolutely critical to the customer's journey. That 1 percent drives her research and attention to other sites that offer content to answer her questions and needs. It's also the 1 percent that will jump-start her journey toward becoming a paying customer.

---

2 "The B2B Buying Journey" – Todd Ebert (Chief Marketing Officer, MultiView)

Sophia doesn't spend all her time sitting at the computer, skimming marketing tips like a robot and commenting on her favorite subreddits: she's an active mom with a full schedule outside the office. She loves trying new lunch spots with friends, finding fun activities for her kids, and going out on date nights with her husband. And just like you, Sophia has her mobile phone at all times. She's checking in to that lunch spot, reading reviews about those activities for her kids, and making reservations for a romantic night out — all through a mobile device.

Sophia's desktop usage hits its peak during her typical work hours. The largest spike in mobile usage typically occurs during the evening hours on her tablet.

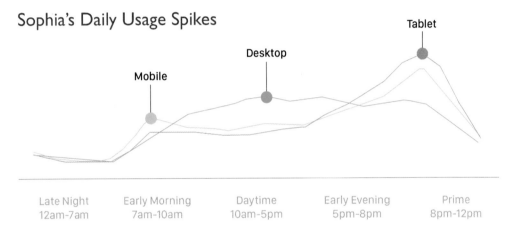

Figure #11: Sophia's daily usage spikes for each main platform

Back at home, Sophia checks her Facebook, watches a few Instagram stories and catches up on the latest in her parenting blogs. Like most moms, there isn't enough time in the day for Sophia.

Let's take a sidebar from Sophia's journey to talk about mobile device usage, because this is a key channel through which Sophia — and your audience — consumes content when they're not at work.

The boom in mobile usage is not over,
it's just different

After the initial blast of smartphone production nearly a decade ago, mobile content fundamentally changed. Within a few years, everything that could be viewed or optimized for a mobile device became extremely valuable for marketers. Users' appetites for mobile content grew.

We spend an enormous amount of time using mobile social apps like Facebook, Snapchat, and Instagram, which rely on content to keep us engaged with each other and with brands. Research from eMarketer projected that time spent per day on mobile would increase by 17 minutes from 2016 to 2018, reaching a total 3 hours and 23 minutes per day.[3] During that same period, time spent on desktop would decrease by 3 minutes, and TV viewing by 10 minutes.

The boom in mobile usage has been a popular strategy consideration for marketers during the last few years. And that's for good reason. Consumers like Sophia spend more time than ever on mobile devices,

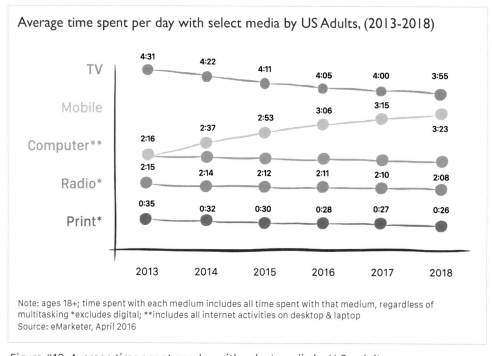

Average time spent per day with select media by US Adults, (2013-2018)

Note: ages 18+; time spent with each medium includes all time spent with that medium, regardless of multitasking *excludes digital; **includes all internet activities on desktop & laptop
Source: eMarketer, April 2016

Figure #12: Average time spent per day with select media by U.S. adults

The trend is showing that more and more time will be spent on mobile and even less on traditional media over the next decade. In a recent study by Nielsen and Google, it was determined that "in-the-moment" type searches are the most popular among users — with 85 percent of smartphone users looking for local information and a whopping 81 percent following up to take action.[4]

---

3 https://www.emarketer.com/corporate/coverage/be-prepared-mobile
4 https://www.thinkwithgoogle.com/consumer-insights/creating-moments-that-matter/

Very quickly, consumers aren't just getting information, they're considering options and often going straight to brick-and-mortar stores to make purchases. In fact, 50 percent of consumers who conduct a local search on their smartphone visit a store within a day, and 18 percent of those searches lead to a purchase within a day. If they're unsure where to eat, nearly 50 percent of users won't even search for a restaurant until within an hour of leaving the house (not surprisingly, that number jumps to almost 60 percent for millennials).[5] And it doesn't stop there. Once at their destination, they're fine-tuning their search to help make better choices on what to eat. Another survey showed that 40 percent of surveyed millennials said they looked up information about their food while in the restaurant![6]

"Consumers today, especially with the technology they have available, they expect immediacy," says Serena Potter, Group Marketing VP at Macy's, in an interview with Think With Google. "I think search is really one of those tools that allows them to quickly find exactly what they're looking for and better understand where it's available."

"More Google searches take place on mobile devices than on computers in 10 countries including the US and Japan."

- Google AdWords Blog

Based on an average of 11 key categories and associated queries, U.S. mobile search is roughly 58 percent of overall search query volume according to Hitwise's "Mobile Search: Topics and Themes" report.[7] The company "examined hundreds of millions of online search queries" across PCs, smartphones and tablets between April 10 and May 7, 2016.

A mini consumer journey:
shopping for school supplies

We're back to Sophia, who's just beginning her customer journey in search of an advanced degree in marketing or a related field that will help her move into the C suite. We're going to experience a mini-customer journey with her, as she realizes that her kids need school supplies.

5 https://www.thinkwithgoogle.com/consumer-insights/i-want-to-go-micro-moments/
6 https://www.thinkwithgoogle.com/consumer-insights/i-want-to-go-micro-moments/
7 http://hitwise.connexity.com/070116_MobileSearchReport_CD_US.html

AWARENESS

After the little ones fought taking a bath, fought putting on pajamas, fought reading a bedtime story, fought going to bed, fought staying asleep — those so-called bundles of joy are finally out for the night, and Sophia has the house to herself. Her husband has long since fallen asleep on their back patio, listening to his favorite music and enjoying a glass of wine. It's early August and school is about to start; Sophia's browsing Facebook when she sees a friend mention the joys and pains of school shopping. Whoops! Sophia's heart drops into her stomach when she suddenly realizes she hasn't even started her own school shopping for the kids.

> **Anna Di Santo**
>
> Back to school shopping starts again! I can't find anything for Noah, it's so hard finding stuff for him! Arlo is all set, though - he is officially ready for 1st grade!
>
> 👍 Like　　　💬 Comment　　　↗ Share

Jumping on her laptop, Sophia begins a broad search in Google for "school supplies." The results in Google are wide and don't offer much help to her (she really doesn't know what she's looking for yet, but ran to Google in a panic). This first search is important, because searchers will quickly narrow the inquiry to find the answers they need. After all, sites listed on the first Google search results page generate 92 percent of all traffic from an average search, according to a report by Chitika Insights.[8] When moving from page 1 to page 2, the traffic dropped by 95 percent, and by 78 percent and 58 percent for the subsequent pages. This means that the average user refines their search rather than continuing past page one of the SERPs.

Sophia quickly calms down and thinks to herself, "I can't get any school supplies if my kids don't have something to put them in. I'll restart my search and find backpacks for them."

---

8 https://chitika.com/google-positioning-value

CONSIDERATION

Now aware of what she's looking for, Sophia begins to consider which option is best for her kids. She narrows her search to "school backpack":

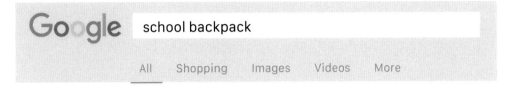

Google | school backpack

All   Shopping   Images   Videos   More

Shop for school backpacks on Google

Backpack, Colton	Samsonite Zalia	Small ClassMate	Pre-K MacKenzie
$18.99	$99.99	$12.99	$16.99
Pottery Barn Kids	Amazon	Target	Jansport
30% price drop	Free Shipping	★★★★☆ (48)	★★★★☆ (4)

School Backpacks - Pottery Barn Kids
https://www.potterybarnkids.com/category/backpacks/u/school ▾
Shop 1000s of **backpacks**, including best-selling bags from top brands. Enjoy our 110% price guarantee, free shipping + earn Rewards on every purchase.
Kids School Backpacks - Patagonia Refugio 28L - Laptop Backpacks

Backpacks - Target
www.target.com/c/backpacks-luggage/ ▾
Items 1 - 24 of 1014 - Shop Target for **backpacks** in a variety of colors, styles and characters. Free Shipping on purchases over $35
Adult backpacks - Kids' Backpacks - SwissGear

Backpacks | Amazon
www.amazon.com/c/backpacks-luggage/ ▾
Items 1 - 24 of 1014 - Shop Target for **backpacks** in a variety of colors, styles and characters. Free Shipping on purchases over $35
Adult backpacks - Kids' Backpacks - SwissGear

Figure #13: Google SERP result for "school backpack"

After quickly scanning page 1 results, she notices options in Google Shopping results, and a few familiar brands stand out within the first few paid and organic listings — Target, Amazon, Pottery Barn and JanSport. She clicks on a few results and browses backpack options, but nothing piques her interest. She's ready to fine-tune her search, again. Both of her kids love animals, specifically, lions. Sophia wants to find backpacks that her kids will enjoy using all year. She narrows her search with a longer-tail keyword phrase: "animal school backpack":

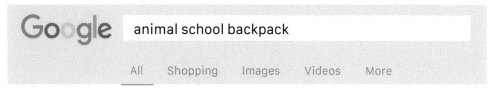

Shop for animal school backpacks on Google

Pre-K Dinosaur	Kitten Toddler	Fox Pre-K Pack	Unicorn Backpack
$29.99	$22.99	$12.99	$16.99
Pottery Barn Kids	Amazon	Target	JanSport
30% price drop	Free Shipping	★★★★☆ (48)	★★★★☆

Images for animal school backpacks on Google

• More images for animal school backpacks

School Backpacks - Pottery Barn Kids
https://www.potterybarnkids.com/category/backpacks/u/school ▾
16' **Animal** Pre-K Dinosaur, Toddler pack **school backpacks**.
Size. Approx 16" x 12" x 5" - Mesh pickets on side

Animal: Backpacks - Target
www.target.com > luggage > backpacks > animal backpacks ▾
Items 1 - 24 of 1014 - Shop Target for **backpacks** in a variety of colors, styles and characters. Free Shipping on purchases over $35

Figure #14: Google SERP result for "animal school backpack"

Just by adding that one descriptive keyword, Sophia's results are much different. Target is still the most familiar brand among these options, and there's even a store close to her house.

She clicks through to check out Target's animal backpacks.

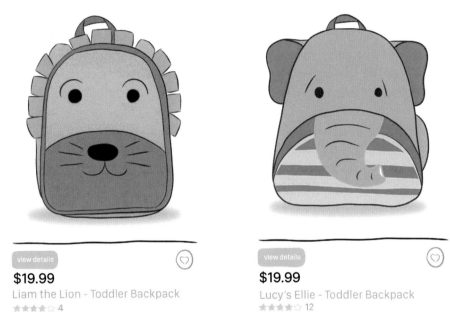

view details ♡
$19.99
Liam the Lion - Toddler Backpack
★★★★☆ 4

view details ♡
$19.99
Lucy's Ellie - Toddler Backpack
★★★★☆ 12

Figure #15: School backpack options for Sophia's kids

DECISION

After reading reviews and comparing prices on competitor websites, Sophia is ready to make a buying decision. She opts to save time and shipping costs by buying online from Target and picking up the backpacks at her favorite Target store.

Target secured Sophia's business because they understood her customer journey. When she conducted her initial searches, they provided answers to her inquiries. As she narrowed her searches, Target was the only brand that had content (or products) related to search queries at every stage of her journey (awareness, consideration and decision). On top of that, they provided a great customer experience by offering Sophia the ability to pick up the products at the store nearby. This is a great step toward making Sophia an advocate for their brand, but she's not there — yet.

ADVOCACY

Sophia doesn't realize it, but she just completed a short customer journey by buying school supplies.[9] Within an hour, she:

• Became aware of school supply options
• Considered which option provided the most benefits for her kids
• Decided on what product to buy

Because Target had content and resources ready for her at the right time, using the correct keywords, Sophia will remember the brand as a trusted resource for school supplies in the future. But she's not an advocate just yet. Sure, she found the product she was looking for easily throughout the customer journey, but her experience didn't solidify any loyalty to the brand. If Target continues to nurture her with more content and related products, Sophia could not only return for more products, but also encourage others to do the same.

9 Keep in mind, B2B buying decisions typically take much longer and involves a more complex process than this B2C example.

"According to Google, on average, your audience completes 68% of their buying decision before contacting any organization."

– CEB Marketing Leadership Council and Google

Sophia embarks on her MBA journey

Like all other customers online, Sophia is in total control of how she shops for products and services — or an advanced degree in business or marketing. Consumers self-educate as quickly and as slowly as they please (depending on their challenges) prior to actually engaging with a sales person or making purchases. Online consumers obtain nearly all the information they need to build trust with a brand and make purchases from their smartphones or laptops.

Sophia may have just completed a short customer journey, but she's unaware of the long one she's about to embark on and oblivious that she will soon be targeted by content that will change the course of her career.

Main Takeaways
& Action Steps

1

What topics or questions do your prospects have before they reach out to you?

2

What "in-the-moment" searches do your customers have when seeking information that relates to your industry?

3

What are the stages of your customers' journeys? What channels and devices do they use during each stage?

CHAPTER II
Sophia enters the awareness stage

Another work day passes; another day feeling less-satisfied as Sophia leaves work. The news on TV is stressful, work is demanding, the future (although not apocalyptic) is uncertain for most. To unwind from the daily pressures, she enjoys listening to talk radio during the long drive home, typically stuck in rush-hour traffic. Today's story:

The Rise of the Online MBA: How Flexible Education Equates to Higher Salaries

Samantha Beacon:

> *Like most millennials, Stephen Reilly was feeling unfulfilled at work. Three years earlier, he had graduated from a four-year university and was now working a corporate job in sales. Like the 70 percent of professionals not engaged at work, according to the 2017 Gallup State of the American Workplace report, Reilly often felt bored, unmotivated and yearning for something more during his 40-plus-hour workweeks.[10]*

Stephen Reilly:

> *I thought after graduating that I'd be able to find a job where I could use my talents and contribute more to the company I was working for. I found myself barely making over $40,000 a year at an entry-level position, where I rarely was able to support any type of strategy. I always dreamed of being an entrepreneur someday, and in this role, I felt stuck and dreaded going to work.*

Beacon:

> *Armed with a desire to climb the corporate ladder more quickly, both so he could have the finances to move out of a place he shared with two roommates and so he could have a chance to obtain a leadership position within the company, Reilly went online to search for flexible learning opportunities. With the intent to keep working while he learned, he found a multitude of online MBA programs, offered by more than 250 schools.[11] Most universities with campuses today also offer online programs, which allow students and professionals like Reilly to learn on their own time.*
>
> *Reilly signed up for Magellan University's online MBA program and graduated in two years. Now, a year after graduation, he's making 50 percent more than his previous salary. He secured a management role that gives him direct access to strategy development at his current company.*

---

10 https://news.gallup.com/reports/178514/state-american-workplace.aspx
11 https://www.usnews.com/education/online-education/mba/rankings

Reilly:

While I was studying, I was able to apply what I learned to my old sales role. I quickly became a top earner among my peers, and once I graduated, I applied for a management position that was open. Typically, it might have taken me five to 10 more years to get that position. With my MBA, I was able to move into my ideal role far more quickly.

Beacon:

Reilly is not alone in an increase in working professionals embracing online schooling for an MBA. A recent survey by Aslanian Market Research and Learning House found more than 90 percent of online MBA students are full-time workers.[12] The average age of a person entering an online MBA program is 33 years old, compared to 27 for on-campus MBA students. A third of online MBA students had financial support from employers, with some employers paying full tuition for the program.

Customer relationship management software company Integrationhard is one such company that offers full reimbursement for graduate expenses to full-time employees. CEO Richard Ross says by supporting full-time team members with tuition reimbursement, the company has seen a dramatic shift in innovation and productivity because of the benefits continued learning provides.

Richard Ross:

Since we implemented the tuition reimbursement program four years ago, we've had more than 50 employees go on to get their graduate degrees. These employees typically move on to leadership roles in the company, and we've seen a dramatic return on investment when tracking performance of not just the graduates, but of the teams they lead. I've talked to some VPs and CEOs of other companies who are hesitant because of the costs and who think their employees might be distracted with school. At Integrationhard, we've seen the exact opposite: We end up increasing sales and see employees who are more engaged at their jobs.

Beacon:

The return on investment for online MBA students is just as substantial. Positions featured in the Bureau of Labor Statistics Occupational Outlook Handbook show that advanced titles often require graduate degrees and have higher starting salaries.

---

12 http://www.learninghouse.com/wp-content/uploads/2016/07/OCS-2016-Report.pdf

There is far more potential for working candidates to advance and earn exponentially more. The Aslanian Market Research and Learning House report shows an average of more than a 22 percent increase in salary after MBA graduation.[13]

MBA students also cite the additional benefit of virtual networking with students around the globe, which may lead to future referrals or the ability to find employment at other desirable companies.

For workers like Reilly who want to advance more quickly or who feel stagnant in their current roles, exploring options like online MBA programs and company reimbursement help to increase not only salary, but overall job satisfaction.

Reilly:

I'm so happy I didn't just resign myself to working my way up on the schedule my company typically allows. Getting my online MBA made my work while I was studying so much more stimulating, and now I'm in a position that will help me when I want to start my own business.

Beacon:

A 2017 survey by the Graduate Management Admission Council found 86 percent of companies worldwide plan to hire recent MBA graduates in 2017, an increase from 79 percent that hired them in 2016.[14] The report also noted that MBA base salaries will increase at or above the rate of inflation in 2017, paving the way for more career growth opportunities for MBA graduates. For Onward & Upward Radio News, I'm Samantha Beacon.

The radio spot sparks the interest of Sophia, who's constantly wondering what the future holds for her career. After looking for ways to climb up the corporate ladder, this radio segment introduces a path that might allow Sophia to reach her professional goals. This type of attention-grabbing content is what makes traditional marketing still so effective.

In addition to listening to the interview on the radio, Sophia notices a digital billboard on her way home advertising Magellan University, which reaffirms her motivation to learn more. Interesting to note, this billboard has been up and on her way home for months, but this is the first time she's noticed it.

---

13 https://www.bls.gov/ooh/business-and-financial/home.htm
14 https://globenewswire.com/news-release/2017/06/20/1026035/0/en/Nearly-9-in-10-Companies-Plan-to-Hire-MBA-Graduates-in-2017.html

Our brains are great filters. When we are ready to receive a message, our brains let the information in. It's one of the best arguments to consistently advertise in the awareness stage to increase your reach and attract new prospects. But we'll get to that later.

Figure #16: Traditional billboard advertisement

Does traditional marketing still matter?

Contrary to what you may have been told lately, traditional marketing is far from dead. At least, not yet anyway. Companies still invest millions of dollars into these mediums, because radio and television reach massive audiences and can still drive a huge amount of revenue to a business.

Various forms of digital advertising are top-of-mind for most marketers these days. But two recent studies from MarketingSherpa and HubSpot suggest that traditional marketing — including print, TV and radio — is still just as important when attracting new customers.[15][16] In fact, some might argue it's more important than digital in the early stages of the customer journey. HubSpot surveyed 1,055 online users in the U.S. and Europe, and found that more people disliked online (digital) advertisements than traditional ads:

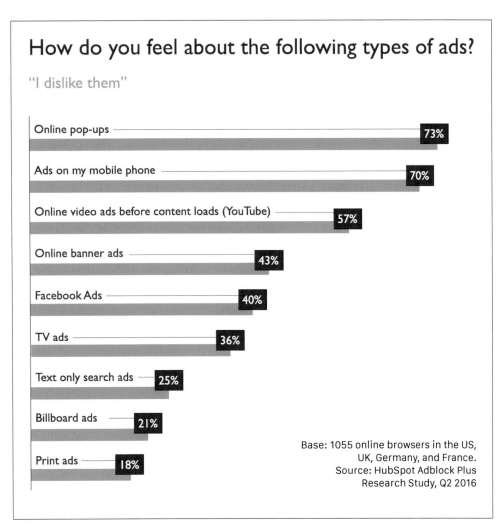

Figure #17: How do users feel about the following types of ads?

15 http://marketingsherpa.com/freestuff/customer-first-study

16 https://research.hubspot.com/reports/why-people-block-ads-and-what-it-means-for-marketers-and-advertisers

Why? Because consumers tend to trust traditional advertising more than digital. That might be surprising for some. After all, we've learned from Jay Baer that digital marketing (specifically, content marketing) is about helping, not selling. As digital marketers, we've made it a point to not produce interruptive content and instead work to establish a trusting relationship with our audience. Among the consumers surveyed in the 2016 MarketingSherpa study, the top five most-trusted ad formats are all traditional media:

Print advertising	Television advertising	Direct mail advertising	Radio advertising	Out-of-home advertising
82% TRUST	80% TRUST	76% TRUST	71% TRUST	69% TRUST

While millennials heavily prefer digital advertisements, the majority of your audience will consume both traditional and digital content. For this reason, it's important to strategize around both.[17]

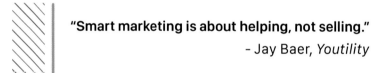

"Smart marketing is about helping, not selling."

- Jay Baer, *Youtility*

Like digital, traditional media is crafted for human interaction. Traditional marketing works to catch as much attention as possible, and entices the audience to act. It's one of the most effective and efficient ways of reaching a massive audience, if you have the budget for it. Billboards, TV ad campaigns, radio spots, newspaper ads, and other traditional outlets ensure that you get the outreach your brand needs, but there isn't much opportunity to nurture your audience down the sales funnel. That's why, of course, digital marketing should always be a part of your strategy. It's essential to blend the power of both traditional and digital marketing, to not only reach a massive audience, but to also lead them through the customer journey.

---

17 https://www.clickz.com/84-percent-of-millennials-dont-trust-traditional-advertising/27030/

Remember, measurement is critical for any marketing strategy. It's imperative that you track the results of your traditional and digital advertising campaigns. To accomplish this, consider using codes in print ads and custom URLs in digital ads to see which campaigns get the best results. That way, you can easily track how much traffic, leads and conversions come from those traditional avenues — and you can determine the successes and failures of these strategies.

Magellan University's radio segment and billboard certainly sparked interest, but it's not going to get Sophia to automatically enroll into MBA courses at the first university she sees. Magellan University still needs to build a relationship with her, and they'll use content as a tool to establish trust.

Stephen Reilly collaborates with Magellan University on influencer content

Back to our story. Magellan University is a popular school located in the northwestern region of the United States. They have a proud history of successful alumni and aren't scared to boast about their bachelor and master's degree programs through their multi-million-dollar marketing campaigns. They've built up a reputation of being authoritative, intellectual and elite among comparable colleges and universities nearby. Because Magellan University is a large school, the website is popular, with strong domain and page authority that generates a lot of traffic each month. With little effort, their content reaches the front pages of SERPs.

Now that Stephen Reilly was interviewed in the radio segment and acted as an advocate for Magellan University's MBA program, the school felt it was a good opportunity to reach out to him and create a related piece of content that would live on the school's website. Stephen agreed to collaborate on the content and distribute it through his network online.

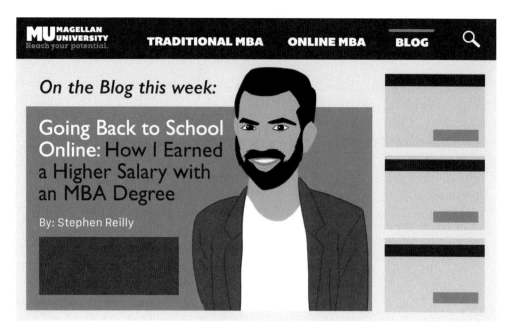

FIGURE #18: Stephen Reilly's collaborative content with Magellan University

Stephen uses some of the notes from his radio spot to create his own new piece of content. The article, "Going Back to School Online: How I Earned a Higher Salary with an MBA Degree," highlights Stephen's success story and delivers a resounding review of the Magellan University MBA program.

Once published, Stephen shares the article on his LinkedIn page to a network of fellow marketing professionals.

He shares it for a few reasons:

1. He's proud of this accomplishment and feels it's beneficial for his professional growth to promote the story.
2. He wants to help his peers and connections in the industry to help them grow.
3. He's an advocate for Magellan University and wants to help promote their MBA program to others.

Guess who else is in Stephen's network of marketing professionals? Sophia. Though she had quickly forgotten about the radio program and billboard when she got home the other day, Stephen's post re-engages her, and she even shares the piece of content to her own professional network, asking if others have thought about pursuing their MBA, too.

Not only does Sophia follow Stephen Reilly from a LinkedIn group, she also recognizes Magellan University from the Onward & Upward Radio News segment. Sophia quickly connects the dots. Magellan University is using influencer marketing to help her become aware of (and interested in) the opportunity to earn an advanced business degree.

What is influencer marketing?

Influence, defined by Oxford Dictionaries, is "the capacity to have an effect on the character, development, or behavior of someone or something, or the effect itself." Influence is a powerful thing – it's the ability to cause an action, to spur a movement or to shape an opinion. In today's digital space, influence holds a more integral role in marketing than ever before.

There isn't just one way or one time to use influencer marketing, as there are multiple stages and touchpoints at each stage of consumers' decision-making processes. Using influencer marketing at each stage of the journey creates a more holistic approach to digital marketing.

According to Adweek, influencer marketing is "a form of marketing that has emerged from a variety of recent practices and studies, in which focus is placed on specific key individuals (or types of individual) rather than the target market as a whole."[18]

To put it simply, influencer marketing is when businesses work with influential people in their industry to produce and promote content to reach a wider audience. And that's exactly what Magellan University and Stephen Reilly are trying to accomplish. As a trusted business expert, Stephen benefits from collaborating on content with Magellan University because he can tap into their audience, further establishing himself as a trusted authority in the industry. For Magellan University, they're able to entice potential students to their MBA program by collaborating with an influencer (who also happens to hold an MBA degree).

However, there's some confusion around influencer marketing: Some businesses think that as long as someone has a large social following, he or she is an influencer. An influencer is actually anyone who can assist your business in getting more clients.

---

18 http://www.adweek.com/digital/10-reasons-why-influencer-marketing-is-the-next-big-thing/

You don't need to get LeBron James to promote your backhoe rental company based out of Jackson, Wyoming. You might, however, want to get a trusted influencer in that industry to talk about the difference between John Deere and Caterpillar equipment. Depending on your industry, influencers might be people with a large following, but others (like our backhoe rental company example) might be a niche blogger who has extensive experience and knowledge on the subject matter — while they might not have the same number of followers, they do have a considerable amount of social capital.

What's social capital? Put it this way: you might have 100,000 followers on Twitter, but if nobody is actively engaging or listening to your posts, what good are the followers? Social capital means that influencers tend to have a following relative to their industry. That might be several thousand followers, RSS subscribers or Facebook "likes". They're frequently retweeted, quoted, interviewed, invited to speak at conferences and may even have written a book or two about the industry.

Stephen Reilly has a large following, and Sophia is one (among many) who saw "Going Back to School Online: How I Earned a Higher Salary with an MBA Degree" in her LinkedIn feed and shared it. Magellan University and Stephen Reilly are telling a story that's easy for Sophia to put together; she's becoming aware of her options to go back to school, and she's ready to learn more.

Main Takeaways
& Action Steps

1

What does your traditional and digital marketing mix look like today? What might you need to add or subtract?

2

What pain points or dreams do your customers have that you can address with awareness-stage content?

3

Who are the influencers in your industry or audience (experts, advocates) who could help expose your brand?

CHAPTER III
Sophia considers her options and searches for related content

Sophia isn't ready to make any decision yet. In fact, she's still not entirely sure what she's looking for. Stephen Reilly gained professional success through hard work and focusing his studies on business and marketing, but will that educational path work the same for Sophia? She's becoming more aware of possible options to go back to school, but there's more research to be done.

> **"Expecting a sale from a new prospect [in the awareness stage] is like proposing marriage on the first date."**
>
> – Sherice Jacob for the Crazy Egg Blog

After reading the article from Stephen Reilly and Magellan University, Sophia is motivated to learn more about what opportunities are available in her marketing career. She's trying to organize what problems there are to solve, get answers to her questions and generally understand what the future might hold for her. She understands that additional education is required to advance her career, but still doesn't fully know her options.

If she were to go back to school, what degree program would make the most sense? What type of job is she actually trying to land? At this point, the only thing Sophia determined is that she would ultimately benefit most from an MBA track, because it would cover her interest in leading a professional team. A master's degree in marketing, or something similar, would provide deep knowledge of the discipline but might not cover the business leadership skills she seeks. In order for her to make an educated decision, she's going back to Google to begin researching her options — and it's up to Magellan University (and their competitors) to put content in front of Sophia to start building a relationship with this prospective student.

Create content
people actually want

The radio spot motivated Sophia to learn more about MBA degrees, but that's not the only way she could have been influenced into beginning her customer journey. You can certainly create a killer blog post or an amazing podcast, but there are other types of content that can accomplish the same goal. In fact, some of the following examples might work better for your audience, depending on your industry and their interests.

*Please note: Each content option has merit of its own and should be judged separately on its value to your content marketing strategy. We don't recommend tackling these unless you have significant resources available. Pick only the ones that you feel confident in creating and will allow you to do a stellar job.

Ideation. It's simple, but not easy.

Many online marketers start to treat headlines and topics like they are writing for a magazine or a newspaper. They use catchy headlines designed to attract the reader's attention to their article. After all, now they know all about their audience and exactly what they want — right? Well, writing headlines for websites is a very different process entirely. Your mindset shouldn't be about being clever — you should be thinking like a searcher.

What is your searcher typing or speaking into the search engines to find information? We can assure you, they're not typing in catchy headlines — they're typing or speaking questions, comparisons and other searches to help them answer questions or solve a problem.

We once worked with a potential client in the solar energy sector. Their blog had titles like this:

- Bringing Solar Curriculum to Schools
- Solar Powered Sounds for the Beach
- Our Customer Love Program
- Giveaways and Gimmicks
- Remodel it Right, Remodel it Green

Although interesting in their own right, these are not titles that potential solar energy customers actually search for in Google.

Titles that match what this company's prospects would search for online would look more like this:

- How much does solar cost?
- How much can I save with solar?
- Can I finance my solar installation?
- Solar vs. electric

How to write headlines for search is difficult for many writers and editors to grasp because they've generally been trained on a different paradigm. And yet, poorly optimized headlines are one of the main reasons content marketing programs stall out. Not writing titles and headlines that speak to what users are actually searching will cause your efforts to fail — you simply won't be found.

Many prospects come to us to help them "fix" their content marketing programs. They've been writing and publishing what they think is great content for six months to a year, yet they haven't seen sufficient results. Along with other issues, almost 100 percent of the time, we find their titles, headlines, subheads and content are not optimized for search engines or for searchers.

Think like a searcher

Using the following ideation tools and concepts will help you think like a searcher. The topics you develop using these tools will come directly from searches that are currently being made in the search engines. By using these techniques, you'll be able to develop content that searchers actually want. You'll also be able to identify what exact titles you should use and where this content fits in the customer journey.

Search engines and searchers have become more sophisticated over the years. Search engines today use machine learning and complex algorithms to identify the intent behind each search query.

Meanwhile, searchers have gone from using a one-or two-word phrase to using full questions and long-tail queries. Smart phones now give searchers the ability to "speak" a search, too — these voice searches are generally longer, as well.

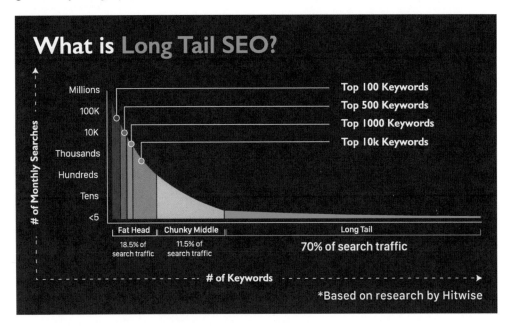

Figure #19: The search demand curve with long-tail SEO (Source: Moz with Hitwise)

If you're still trying to focus on a single priority keyword and optimizing for that narrow focus, you're missing the point. According to research from Moz, more than 70 percent of the traffic you earn for any given page will come from long-tail keywords you didn't try to optimize for.[19]

With the Google Hummingbird update in 2013, the algorithm started to become much smarter in identifying what people want to find when they search. This update incorporated semantic principles into the algorithm. It allowed the searcher to see answer-box and other quick results directly in the SERP.

---

19 https://moz.com/beginners-guide-to-seo/keyword-research

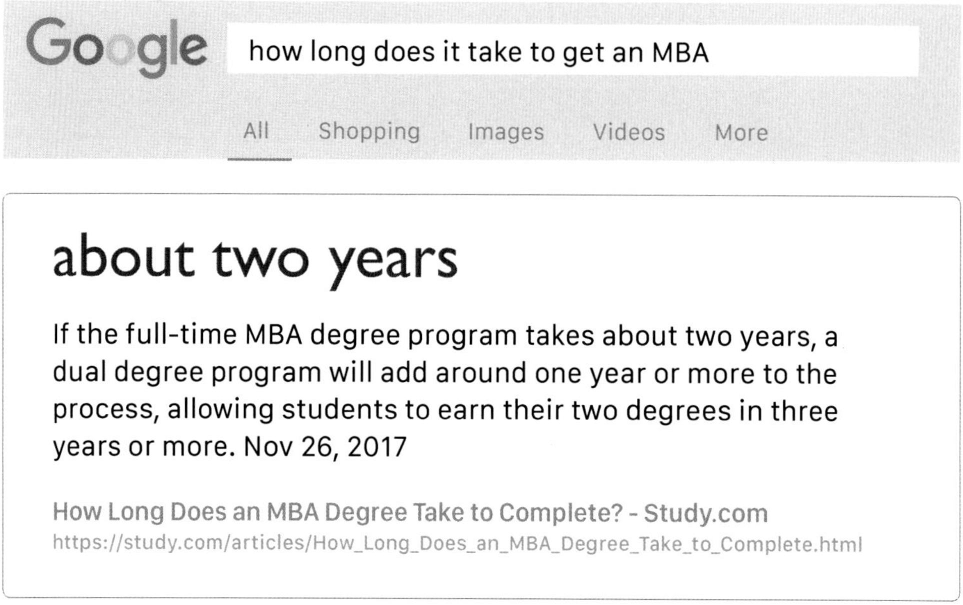

Google   how long does it take to get an MBA

All   Shopping   Images   Videos   More

about two years

If the full-time MBA degree program takes about two years, a dual degree program will add around one year or more to the process, allowing students to earn their two degrees in three years or more. Nov 26, 2017

How Long Does an MBA Degree Take to Complete? - Study.com
https://study.com/articles/How_Long_Does_an_MBA_Degree_Take_to_Complete.html

Figure #20: Example of an answer box in the Google SERPS

Semantic search goes beyond the meanings of separate, distinct keywords to deliver SERP results based on the intent behind a searcher's queries. This process takes the broader search context into account — even when the user intent is implied rather than explicit. To put it simply, intent is everything nowadays. Search intent allows a publisher to determine exactly where the searcher is in the customer journey and to create appropriate content that directly matches their intent.

Pay attention to the natural searches happening right now. Support your priority keywords with stemmed, thematic, tangential, close variants and other topical phrases. Long-tail keyword searches have become more and more important with the advent of voice search.

So, what are long-tail keyword searches? They're the multi-word search queries that may have very low individual search volume on their own but, when combined as a group of related searches, provide an enormous total search demand. Their name comes from the "long-tail" of the so-called "search demand curve" — a graph that plots all keywords by their search volumes.[20] In the aggregate, long-tail terms will drive more organic traffic than one- to two-word, priority or "head" terms.

---

20 https://ahrefs.com/blog/long-tail-keywords/

"Always be looking for ways to add value — not what you think is valuable, but what the customer finds valuable. Every marketing initiative at each stage in the funnel should continually ask 'what can we do to make this even better?'"

- Sherice Jacob for Neil Patel

Fit content into each stage
of the customer journey

Potential customers can visit your site at any stage of the customer journey. At this stage, Sophia wants to further her search after learning about the higher salaries that MBA graduates earn. She's starting her search near the top of the sales funnel and needs more information to refine it.

The value of an effective customer journey is a sum of its parts. You need to publish content for every stage of the journey to capture and connect with prospects however and whenever the search.

"Then, with a well-curated path to purchase in place, each content piece within the journey serves a need, independently and collectively, regardless the point of entry. The end result guides people to the right resources, while also quickly and seamlessly answering their questions."

- Katrina Pfannkuch for Kapost

As you create content,
focus on these topic categories:

- Answering Questions
- Price/Cost
- Versus/Comparisons
- Top/Best
- Problems/Issues
- Reviews

Answering questions

According to data from Jumpshot, 8 percent of search queries are phrased as questions.[21] In this stage of the journey — consideration — you must resist the temptation to emphasize your brand or sales pitch. The searcher is looking for information, so create content that informs, teaches and guides the person deeper into the journey. Your job in this stage is to educate, not persuade or sell (that comes later). The searcher can certainly be influenced in this stage, but they're not ready to buy.

For the searcher, this stage is all about discovery. What are the opportunities, what are the possibilities, will they fit into my lifestyle, and is it something that I can achieve over time? You need to prove to the searcher that your solution is worth considering by showing them you are knowledgeable, by being helpful, and by providing the best answer. By answering the right questions at the right time, you put yourself into a position of strength against your competition. You build trust through content that's factual, backed by research and, most importantly, useful.

As you develop top-of-funnel content, ensure you publish it not only on your site, but also in as many appropriate channels as possible. You want to cast as wide a net as you can. Your goal should be to make your content accessible, as you never know where or when the searcher will come in contact with your content.

Price/Cost

Your content should also cover the cost of your product or service and related information, since these questions will eventually come up in a search query. A price/cost search from your audience represents a very high search intent. It's further along in the customer journey, and it could be the last step prior to the searcher making a purchase-decision or becoming a qualified lead.

Price/cost searches that Sofia might enter include:

- How much does it cost to get your MBA?
- How much does a master's degree at X college cost?
- Is the cost of an MBA worth it?
- How much does an MBA cost on average?

---

21 https://moz.com/blog/state-of-searcher-behavior-revealed

Versus/Comparisons

Searchers compare before they buy. Still in the consideration stage, the user is trying to find more information about how their potential choice might stack up against others. A quick versus or comparison search can help them get the information they need. Think of your own habits as a consumer — how often do you compare products or services before you buy?

By providing information about your competition, you are also building trust. Many businesses are afraid to publish this kind of content because it seems to invite the consumer to go elsewhere. But it's important to remember that the user is on your site reading the comparisons rather than being on another competitor's site. Having the potential customer on your site gives you the opportunity to move them further through the customer journey with a call-to-action.

Versus/comparison searches that Sofia might enter include:

- Online MBA vs traditional classroom course
- Online MBA vs part time MBA
- Harvard vs Yale vs Princeton vs Stanford MBA programs

The content that supports these searches might be a table of features and benefits, as well as comparison charts that help the user easily see and understand their needs and compare them across possible solutions. In Sophia's journey, cost comparisons and financial option comparisons will also help move her through the journey.

Top/Best

Top or best content gives the searcher even more confidence during the consideration stage, as you're providing points of reference that can ultimately lead to a decision. Face it, most of us are lazy. A list of the best choices saves us research time and presents a number of options that can be more quickly explored. Top or best content is easy-to-digest and usually performs really well.

Top/best searches that Sofia might enter include:

- Best online MBA programs
- Top MBA programs/schools
- Best ways to pay for your MBA
- Best ways to finance your MBA
- Top reasons to get your MBA

Problem/Issue

Every business has inherent problems or issues, and it's best to be fully transparent about them. After all, users will probably uncover negative issues as they research and consider their options. Transparency builds trust. Write about your problems, how you have addressed them and why you are the best choice in spite of any problems.

Problem/issue searches that Sophia might enter include:

- Is an MBA worth it?
- Percentage of students that complete MBA degrees
- Are online MBAs recognized?
- Is MBA debt worth the degree?

We'll look more closely at the last kind of consideration content – reviews – in chapter 13.

How do you come up with these ideas?

At this point, you might be saying to yourself, "Well, that's neat. But how the hell do you come up with the topic and headline examples?" And to this we say, don't worry. There's a tool for that, too. Here's a list of areas and tools that our team uses every day. We've found them all to be effective in doing research and in creating great content.

Your own organization

The best place to start your ideation process is within your own organization. You have people that are in direct contact with prospects and current customers on a daily or regular basis. They are hearing first-hand about problems, and they are exposed to the questions being asked every day. You want to find out what they get asked every day.

Sales

Sales people hear objections every day, and the objections they hear should be answered online. Answering sales questions online can help keep users from turning away. After all, 67 percent of a customer's decision is complete before a buyer even reaches out to sales.[22]

Customer service

Want to know what problems your customers are facing? Ask your customer service staff. Then, create content that addresses those problems and issues. Not only does being transparent foster more trust, it gives you more control over the narrative.

Online chat

Analyzing your online chat is a great way to discover what content you are missing on your site. If someone is asking a question in chat, that means you haven't addressed it in content on the site. Chat data is often something companies miss completely, but it's a wealth of information to help guide you to more content you should add to your site.

Site search

Like online chat, search queries done on your site are indicators that you don't have the content the user is looking for or they can't find it. If the content is missing, create it. If it's there, ask yourself why the user couldn't find it and determine if you can fix that.

Admissions

For higher education, this is one of the most important areas to draw content ideas from. A prospective student is far along in their student journey by the time they are communicating with your admissions team. The questions you hear in this stage are extremely important to your new-start ratio. Have you answered all these questions in your content?

Auto suggest

Do you notice when you're typing in a search query in Google, that it auto completes your search? It isn't always right, but it does provide useful variations of your search. Use this to find what people are searching for in and around the phrases that are important to you. Just start typing in your query and see what Google offers up in addition to your search. What do these suggested searches tell us?

22 https://www.siriusdecisions.com/blog/three-myths-of-the-67-percent-statistic

Users themselves are typing in these phrases, so they are great indicators of what content to write.

The next step in this process is to do a search on each query that came up. Look at the search results page to see if any website or competitor is addressing that exact search with their headline or in their description. If not, this is an opportunity to develop an exact-match piece of content that will have a great chance of ranking number one. We've experimented with this theory a number of times and have results to prove the concept.

For example, the search "restaurants near the Mesa Convention Center" was not addressed, so we created content with that exact title on the site arizonatourism.com. The article ranks on the first page of the SERP and it has been in positions 1 through 6 since 2014. Note that the article was published in 2014 and has never been updated. There is ranking power in producing content that searchers are actively searching for, and matching the title to the search query is one of the easiest ways to get your content to rank. The title matches the searcher's query exactly, and the description highlights the content's relevance to the query, as well.

Restaurants Near the Mesa Convention Center - Arizona Tourism

https://arizonatourism.com > Arizona Blog ▼

Jan 12, 2014 - A list of great restaurants near The Mesa Convention Center based on their ascending distance from the facility

Figure #21: Example of Google's SERP preview

While you're on that search results page, look at the related searches at the bottom. Related searches offer more semantically related ideas.

For example:

Searches related to restaurants near the mesa convention center

downtown mesa restaurants on main	fast food near me
best restaurants mesa az	texas roadhouse
best restaurants in mesa az 2016	olive garden
tempe marketplace restaurants	buffalo wild wings

Figure #22: Example of Google's related searches

YouTube

Owned by Google, YouTube has a similar search feature. As the premier video search engine, YouTube is a perfect place to come up with video and "how-to" ideas, and videos often show up in Google searches, as well. For example, Sophia might search, "How do I choose the right MBA student loan?" She would find this as the top video result:

How Do I Choose The Right MBA Student Loan? | The GMAT Club

https://gmatclub.com/.../how-do-i-choose... ▼
May 15, 2015 - Uploaded by CommonBrand

There are two types of **student loads**: federal and private. U.S. citizens and permanent residents are eligible to...

▶ 2:36

Figure #23: Example of video content found in Google's SERPs

Keyword Planner

Previously known as AdWords, Google Ads is an advertising platform that includes a free tool called Keyword Planner. Designed to help you plan paid search campaigns, Keyword Planner can also be used to discover additional keywords and phrases you can target with your content. Start by adding your priority keywords, and build longer phrases based on what Google returns in the tool. Look for synonyms, keyword variants, topics and themes. Focus on long-tail terms, as they might be good titles or subheadings for your content.

This tool highlights the competitive nature of the keywords and also the estimated volume of monthly searches. We've learned over time not to pay too much attention to the number of monthly searches. Take those numbers with a grain of salt. Some of our content pages have received multiple thousands of visits, even when their search volume estimates show in the low hundreds.

Here's an example:

Keyword Search Volume Estimates vs. Actual Traffic Numbers

How it works:

<Title>	🔍

Keyword Term 1	Search Volume Estimator	**Actual**
Keyword Term 2		**Views**

Examples:

Waterfall vs. Agile: Which is the Right Development Methodology for Your Project?	🔍

Waterfall vs Agile	1,600	**93,000+**
Agile vs Waterfall	2,400	

.NET vs. Java: How to Make Your Pick	🔍

Java vs. .Net	390	**71,000+**
Net vs. Java	20	

What Characeristics Make Good Agile Acceptance Criteria?	🔍

Agile Acceptance Criteria	170	**53,000+**
Acceptance Criteria Agile	50	

Figure #24: Example of search volume estimators (Source: Vertical Measures)

Search Console

This resource is an extension of Google Analytics. It adds a layer of data not available in the analytics tool. You can learn what search queries users are searching to find your content.

Search Query	Clicks	Impressions	CTR
	37,815 % of total: 100%	**2,642,133** % of total: 78.38%	**1.43%** % of total: 1.12%
1. (other)	**24,835** (65.67%)	**616,766** (65.67%)	4.03%
2. vertical measures	**1,089** (2.88%)	**1,881** (0.07%)	57.89%
3. h1 tag	**608** (1.611%)	**7,396** (0.28%)	8.22%
4. h1 tags	**293** (0.77%)	**2,420** (0.09%)	12.11%
5. video marketing services	**196** (0.52%)	**11,891** (0.45%)	1.65%
6. h1 tags seo	**180** (0.48%)	**1,196** (0.05%)	15.05%
7. content marketing services	**164** (0.43%)	**16,002** (0.61%)	1.02%
8. google adwords updates 2017	**164** (0.43%)	**894** (0.03%)	18.34%
9. broken links seo	**130** (0.34%)	**1,105** (0.04%)	11.76%
10. instagram vs facebook ads	**127** (0.34%)	**216** (0.01%)	58.80%

Figure #25: Google Analytics dashboard

Google Alerts

You can set up alerts to monitor interesting new content on the web. Just add your keywords or topics you want to be alerted to and the frequency of the updates (http://www.google.com/alerts). Let Google do the heavy lifting for you. Once the alert is set up you can receive updates at different frequencies — daily, weekly and so on. Use this tool to monitor branded terms, support reputation management and see when your business or your competition is mentioned online.

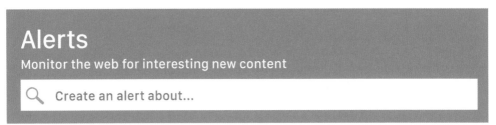

Figure #26: Google Alerts preview

Answer Sites

Answer sites provide you two opportunities for content ideation. The first is to answer the questions being asked and interject your point of view. The second is to understand what questions are being asked and determine if there are content gaps based on those inquiries.

Yahoo! Answers

Users submit questions to the site that are answered by the online community. To filter out spam, Yahoo uses a point system to rank the best answers. You can browse by category and see what questions your audience is asking. If you can't find what you're looking for in the categories, you can always do a keyword search. With the volume of users and the number of questions catalogued, there's a good chance you'll find questions being asked about your product, service or niche industry.

The search query works like Google auto-complete and shows examples of questions users are asking. Are you addressing these questions in your content?

Is an online MBA |

Is an online MBA taken seriously?

is an online mba in health care management worth it?

Is an online MBA degree from Northeastern University worth pursing?

How good **is an online mba**?

What exactly **is an ONLINE MBA** degree?

Is an online MBA worth it? 10 points for bes answer..?

How valuable **is an online MBA**?

Figure #27: Yahoo! Answers suggestion example (Source: Yahoo! Answers)

Quora

This is another answer site similar to Yahoo Answers. It returns results in the same auto-complete fashion:

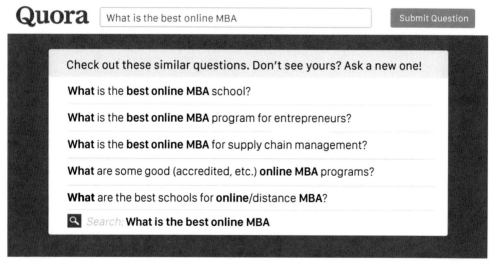

Figure #28: Quora search suggestion example (Source: Quora)

Remember, a prospect can hit your site anywhere in the customer journey. If you have an answer to a common or popular question, you might just snag a lead out of someone else's funnel just by having the best answer.

Business-Focused Websites

LinkedIn

Most people reading this book right now have a profile on LinkedIn, and it's always amazing to find out that so many never use the platform to market their brand. By joining a number of groups, you can discover what other companies are writing about and what other colleagues are discussing.

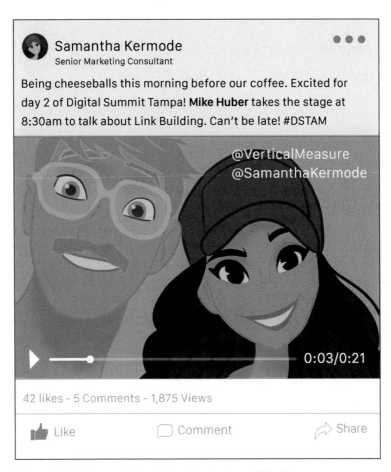

Figure #29: Mike and Sam Video Content on LinkedIn

You can use this channel to extend your audience reach and potentially get traffic back to your site. LinkedIn opened their platform about 2 years ago to allow users to publish unique content and Twitter-like updates. The advantage of publishing on LinkedIn is their rather large, business-focused audience. As always, video content generates the best engagement, and sometimes the content is very easy to produce.

We were in Tampa, Florida at a Digital Summit doing a half-day workshop and produced a quick video update of Samantha Kermode and Mike Huber walking into the conference. The post quickly received almost 1,900 views and was one of the most engaged pieces of content related to that conference — not because the video quality was so great, but because it was timely, relevant to our LinkedIn connections and stirred up conversations with others.[23] LinkedIn also just added audio messaging that you can record straight from your smartphone, similar to voicemail. If you are a B2B company, strongly consider using this platform for content marketing. LinkedIn is the place to network professionally, without ever needing to leave your office.

SlideShare

LinkedIn's content hosting service boasts 80 million users and 18 million content uploads. Here, you'll find a plethora of professional presentations from your competition and other experts. Check out what people in your industry are publishing to determine if they are covering content that you are missing.

Figure #30: SlideShare content examples (Source: SlideShare)

Online Tools

There are a number of online tools to help you discover keywords and topics. We have a few favorites, but there are many more to choose from online, including both paid and free tools.

---

23 https://www.linkedin.com/feed/update/urn:li:activity:6435588036230287360/

AnswerThePublic

Enter your keywords and the tool will return topic results sorted as questions and by preposition. You can organize your results as a visualization or as a list that you can export. This is a great tool for researching a high volume of questions quickly. For example, a search for "online MBA" returned 55 questions and 65 prepositions — this would be very useful information to have if you were targeting Sophia in her customer journey.

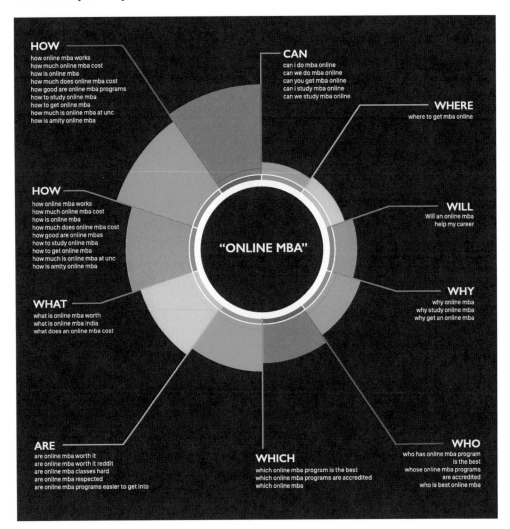

Figure #31: Sample AnswerThePublic results for "online MBA"

Online MBA with

- online mba without prerequisites
- online mba with aacsb accreditation
- online mba with concentration in information systems
- online mba with highest acceptance rate
- online mba with real estate concentration
- online mba with project management
- online mba with concentration in finance
- online mba with gmat

- online mba with concentration in healthcare
- online mba with data analytics
- online mba with hr concentration
- online mba with accounting concentration
- online mba with residency
- online mba with low gpa
- online mba with healthcare concentration
- online mba without gmat
- online mba with gmat waiver

Figure #32: Sample list of prepositions from the same AnswerThePublic search

Your competition

As always, you'll want to consider what content your competition is creating. Are they ranking for keywords that are important to you? If so, have you analyzed their content? Can you publish something better?

A good way to find out what your competition is writing about is to crawl their website. Rather than paging through their website, you can download all their links and learn titles, H1 tags, descriptions and other information from the website crawl. Our favorite tool for this is Screaming Frog.[24] With it, you can crawl up to 500 pages with the free version and unlimited pages with the subscription.

You have your ideas. Now what?

You want to publish content that your audience is searching for at each stage of the customer journey. Use the tools and resources listed in this chapter to discover the biggest content gaps and opportunities for your organization and customers, whether you're coming up with new ideas or refreshing older content already on your site.

What type of content works best?

For now, long-form articles tend to perform better in search engines than thinner content. Articles that average approximately 1,800 words show up most often in the first position in Google.[25] It seems counter-intuitive to be creating long-form content when the average user spends less than a minute on a webpage. That's not the case if you clearly communicate value to the user and structure the content to help people find the information they want.

---

24 https://www.screamingfrog.co.uk/seo-spider/
25 http://backlinko.com/search-engine-ranking

"Users often leave web pages in 10 to 20 seconds, but pages with a clear value proposition can hold people's attention for much longer. To gain several minutes of user attention, you must clearly communicate your value proposition within 10 seconds."

– Nielsen Norman Group

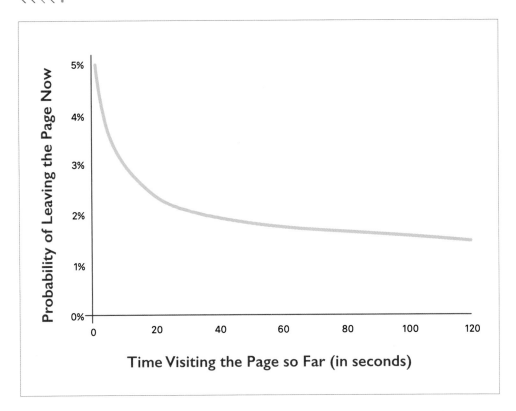

Figure #33: The first 10-20 seconds are critical in a user's decision to stay or to bounce (Source: Nielsen Norman Group)

If your long-form content looks like homework — that is, all text and nothing else — chances are you will lose the potential customer. But, if you break up the content with graphics, tables, images, bulleted lists, numbered lists and video along with bold headers and subheads, it will allow the user (and search engines) to easily skim the information and find what's most valuable to them. We call it "content chunking" and it's a standard part of the formatting in our 10x content.

Rand Fishkin, now CEO of SparkToro, created the term "10x content" during a Moz Whiteboard Friday video.[26] Rand's premise is that there is so much content being published online that it is hard to stand out. In order for your content to stand out, it needs to be 10 times better than the top 10 search results for your particular keyword focus.

According to Rand, 10x content must:

- Have great user interface (UI) and user experience (UX) on any device.
- Be high in quality, trustworthy, useful, interesting and remarkable. Your content doesn't have to be all of those but some combination of them.
- Be considerably different in scope and in detail from other works that are serving the same visitor or user intent.
- Create an emotional response. I want to feel awe. I want to feel surprise. I want to feel joy, anticipation or admiration for that piece of content in order for it to be considered 10x.
- Solve a problem or answer a question by providing that comprehensive, accurate, exceptional information or resources.
- Deliver content in a unique, remarkable and pleasurable style or medium.

We would add that 10x content must also:

- Load quickly on any device, especially mobile.
- Have images, graphics, embedded video and other content chunking elements.
- Focus on one particular theme. It should not be a long list of unrelated items — the search engines will be confused and your article won't rank.

---

26 https://moz.com/blog/how-to-create-10x-content-whiteboard-friday

We've talked mostly about new content, but don't forget the opportunity to refresh content that you've already published. We've been doing this on our own website with great success. Consider the example below.

We had an existing post about the cost of content marketing, with a headline that wasn't in the form of a question. Using the techniques outlined in this chapter, we discovered a number of questions prospects were asking about content marketing. We changed the headline and the six subheads into questions, based on our research. The results were amazing. We not only own the top result for the new headline, but also for six related keyword phrases found in the article.

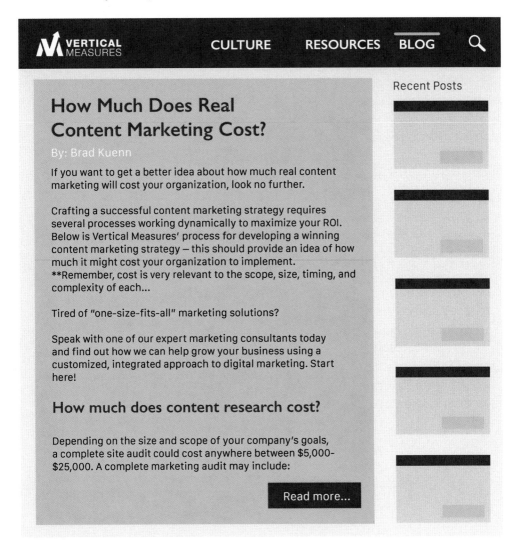

Figure #34: How Much Does Real Content Marketing Cost?

Keyword Phrase	Rank
How Much Does Real Content Marketing Cost? (Article title)	1
How much does content research cost?	1
How much does a content strategy cost?	1
How much does content promotion cost?	1
How much for content marketing education and workshops?	1
How much does content optimization cost?	1
How much does content development cost?	1

Figure #35: Keyword rankings after optimizing content for long-tail searches

Notice how the keywords in each question support the main headline of the article. Try for yourself. Search for these headlines, and you'll notice Vertical Measures owns the top result or "answer box" (for now, at least).

Content Calendar

Now you've got a bunch of amazing content ideas. How do you prioritize them? How much should you publish in a month? Who is going to implement all that content? Where do you manage all these tasks and ideas?

After ideation, the next step is to put together a content calendar that captures and helps you plan out all the ideas you've researched. A content calendar (sometimes known as an editorial calendar) is a crucial part of your strategy. It serves as a road map for the months ahead to ensure your content is planned and optimized to meet business goals, targeting the right audience and helping your contributors, stakeholders and distribution channels work in concert.

A well-planned content calendar will allow you to:

- Coordinate publication with relevant events and business milestones
- Manage production and promotion resources
- Improve brainstorming, research and optimization
- Build on and cross-promote existing or future content
- Identify important metrics and track your content's results

Vertical Measures created a content calendar template to help get you started in your planning for the year.

Download the free calendar template here: **vert.ms/content-calendar**

Main Takeaways
& Action Steps

1

What content types from this chapter are you creating today? What types of content are you missing?

2

Are your titles optimized for the way customers actually search?

3

What existing content do you have that could be a good candidate for 10x optimization?

CHAPTER IV
Sophia refines her search

Let's get back to our protagonist. Sophia starts her research with a lot of conversational or long-tail searches and bounces from competing sites back to the search results. She starts with "How do I advance my marketing career," but after researching, reading content and narrowing her options, she ends up searching, "What can you do with an MBA?"

As she's typing in the latter search, she's presented with Google Suggest options and "What can you do with an MBA in Marketing" catches her eye.

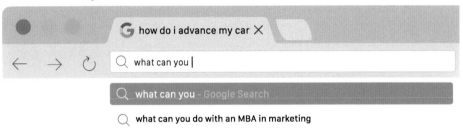

Figure #36: Google search bar example

She thinks, "That's actually something I want to know more about than just earning an MBA degree," and uses the suggestion. The results pull a variety of content:

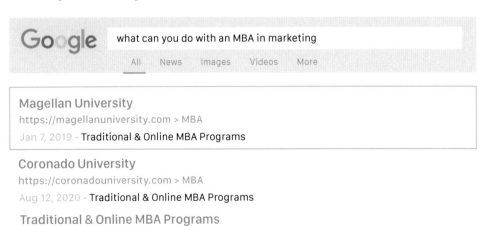

Figure #37: Sample SERP Result with Magellan University, Coronado University, etc.

How'd this content
show up in the SERPs?

The only constant is change. This age-old phrase could not align with the SEO landscape more closely if it tried. Search engine algorithms will never cease to evolve, with their sole purpose being to yield the most helpful, relevant results possible to users. Strategies that worked yesterday could become obsolete by next week. Keeping up with and adapting to algorithm changes can feel incredibly daunting and, at times, impossible.

But there are a few universal truths webmasters and marketers can take solace in:

- Quality will always supersede quantity.
- Businesses will be forced to provide the best answer, rather than a sales pitch.
- Content optimization and improvement for search ranking is never complete.

As technology continues to evolve with innovations like voice search, artificial intelligence and machine learning, it's important to take a step back to understand how we even got to this point. Not so long ago, Google made the conscious decision to crack down on some unethical tactics being utilized throughout the web. These tactics were manipulations of the fundamental principles set by Google. Unfortunately, the real victims were the users. People were stumbling through hollow, useless search results more and more frequently. They were coming across sites and pages that ended up containing almost nothing of true value. Thin, weak and duplicate content became widespread. Spammy backlinks were sprouting up like weeds, and obnoxious, irrelevant advertisements were suffocating the user experience.

By 2011, Google had had enough. Without much warning, they put their massive foot down. Starting with what's commonly known as the Panda update, Google patched up their algorithm to drastically devalue and lower the ranking of countless websites that were trying to get away with minimal word-count, low-quality content and high ad-to-content ratios.[27]

---

27 https://www.searchenginejournal.com/google-algorithm-history/panda-update/

The Panda update sent quite a shockwave throughout the digital landscape. We're sure some of you marketers reading this just got a cold-chill down your spine. Us too.

But Google didn't stop there. In 2012, the company dropped another significant bombshell with their Penguin update.[28] The intent of this algorithm adjustment was to force websites to clean up their deceptive backlink profiles.

The Penguin update penalized:

- Links **on** your website that lead to spammy or irrelevant content
- Links **to** your website from another source that was either paid for or requested by you
- Links **to** your website from sites that are considered "low-quality" or spam
- Excessive links **to** your website from sites with unrelated or irrelevant subject matter

After the dust settled from the Panda and Penguin updates, the effects were eye-opening, to say the least. Companies and webmasters alike were left frantically scrambling to fix their sites in an effort to get their precious rankings back. But, in their typical perfectionist fashion, Google knew they couldn't just stop there. There will always be room for improvement.

In 2013, they decided to throw out the old playbook and design a completely new search algorithm. Sticking with the theme of cute creatures, this algorithm would be commonly referred to as Hummingbird. The purpose behind this drastic update was to better adapt to the way the world was searching for information. The world was (and still is) now searching for information in a much more conversational way. This primarily came about as a result of increasing consumer search sophistication and people using "voice search" through intelligent assistants built-in to their smartphones and devices.

Some of the most well-known voice assistants are Apple's Siri, Google Assistant, Amazon's Alexa, and Microsoft's Cortana.

---

28 http://www.mainstreethost.com/blog/what-is-google-penguin-update/

More than ever before, Google wanted to truly understand the meaning behind the words and the intent of the entire query being searched as a whole. As an example, if a person asked a question looking for specific types of restaurants "near me," Google understands they most likely want options within a few-mile radius of their current location and therefore prioritizes results that fit that expectation, instead of giving them a general listing of restaurants sprawling across the entire city.

As 2015 approached, Google also realized that mobile would eventually surpass desktop as the most widely used medium for search — sooner, rather than later. In preparation for this trend, Google knew that high-speed and functionality would be crucial for the mobile experience to continue its growth path.

Google's designers
went back to the drawing board

Accelerated Mobile Pages

To serve mobile speed, Google came up with a solution known as Accelerated Mobile Pages (commonly referred to as AMP, for short).[29] AMP pages were designed to load mobile pages with lightning quick speed, almost instantly. A simplified way to look at AMP pages is as a basic, stripped-down form of HTML that supports fast load times.

With this mobile-focused AMP rollout, Google made it painfully obvious that sites must be "mobile-friendly." Those who ignore or deny this trend will witness their rankings diminish, yet again, in the name of providing the most relevant information people are searching for with supersonic speed.

Answer box

In 2016, Google slowly unveiled another new, significant feature on the search results page to continue its quest of enhancing the search experience. This feature is known as the "answer box." Referenced earlier in our book, the answer box is a huge win for search users because it provides immediate answers to many simple questions without requiring the effort of having to click-through to the actual site and navigate through the page to find an answer. Website owners seem to have mixed reactions.

---

29 https://moz.com/blog/accelerated-mobile-pages-whiteboard-friday

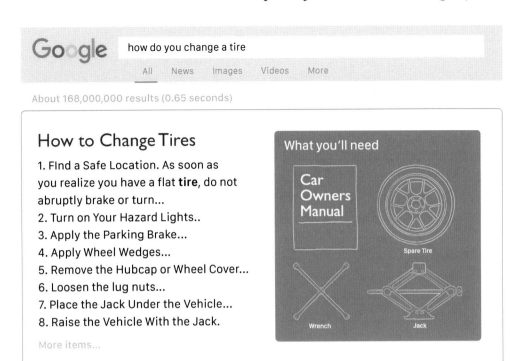

Figure #38: Example of an Answer Box in the Google SERPs

Some have found the answer box puts them above their competitors in "position zero" on page one of the search results, leading to more clicks on their sites from people who want additional information. Meanwhile, others have felt that sometimes the answer box provides the answer in its entirety, making the need to click on to their actual site unnecessary.

Lucky for website owners, Google offers options to overcome this concern. In many cases, Google will allow a call-to-action to be displayed beneath or within the answer box itself. Some answer boxes will also even display additional information, recent news and updates from the site being featured. All of these possible options may encourage searchers to click-through to the actual websites from the answer box.

The key takeaway when it comes to Google's answer box is that they do not appear by accident. Google pulls this information specifically from sites that provide better content than their competitors and use the correct structure and Schema.org markup.[30] There are a few more guidelines that apply in unique circumstances, but those are the basic elements it takes to win the coveted position zero.

RankBrain

Continuing its pursuit of setting trends and pushing the technological envelope, Google also developed an artificial intelligence machine known as RankBrain. This algorithm learning system helps Google more accurately process search queries and provide the most relevant search results possible to its users. For example, if RankBrain encounters a phrase or term it is not familiar with, it will make its best guess to interpret and show results based upon similar words and phrases. Then it will display and filter results based upon all of the previous data it has accumulated on that particular topic.

To be more specific, according to SEO Strategist Matthew Capala, "RankBrain converts the textual contents of search queries into 'word vectors,' also known as 'distributed representations,'" which are close to each other in terms of linguistic similarity. "RankBrain attempts to map this query into words — or 'entities' (clusters of words) — that have the best chance of matching it," Capala explains.

The concept of RankBrain might not sound too different from how Google processed information in the past. On the contrary, it has changed the algorithms significantly. In the past, Google would use over 200 hand-coded factors to rank websites — a highly manual process of testing and implementation. But now, as RankBrain's machine learning capabilities process more and more information about searchers' intent and how words relate to each other, it has the ability to place an incremental emphasis on a specific mixture of the core algorithms to achieve the best results possible based on each unique search query.[31] Yes, these are indeed crazy times we live in, and machine learning will only continue to advance Google's sophistication and semantic understanding.

Link building is still a top factor in Google's algorithm

Mentioned with the Penguin update, backlinks are still one of the top factors (if not the top) that Google's algorithm takes into account when ranking sites — when done correctly.

---

30 https://www.searchenginejournal.com/how-to-optimize-your-site-for-googles-answer-box/166084/
31 Capala, Matthew (2016-09-02). "Machine learning just got more human with Google's RankBrain".

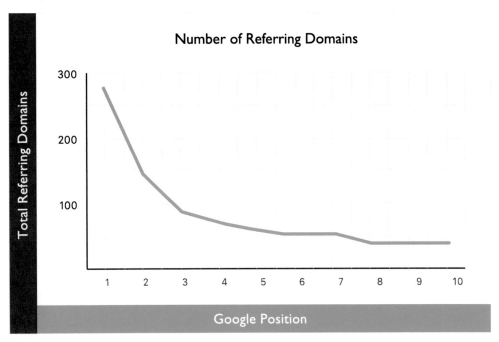

Figure #39: Referring domain's impact on Google ranking (Source: Backlinko.com)

What does it mean to acquire backlinks "correctly?" Well, there are many different factors and criteria that play into that, but the following are some of the main guidelines:

Earn links

Don't pay for them. Seriously. Since the Penguin update in 2012, Google has gotten really good at sniffing out spammy links. If someone is blatantly paying for links or acquiring links that appear to link to any and all types of websites, regardless of industry, Google will quickly recognize it and site rankings will eventually suffer. Basically, if you question whether a link opportunity makes sense or if Google will like it, the safe answer is, "probably not."

Maintain link diversity

Link diversity is achieved in two ways. First, the vast majority of backlinks should not all come from one website or source. Ideally, they should be spread out among a variety of sites, especially ones pertaining to your site's specific industry. Second, you should use different methods to acquire backlinks: guest posting on relevant sites, seeking out unlinked brand mentions, replacing broken links, collaborating with influencers to share content on their social media networks and, most importantly, create amazing, high-quality content that people will naturally want to link to. There are countless other strategies out there to acquire strong backlinks, but these are some of the most common methods.

Reciprocal linking

Just as important as it is to acquire a large volume of high-quality backlinks pointing to a site, it's equally important to link to other, authoritative pages on external websites. Google will raise an eyebrow if a site has hundreds or thousands of backlinks pointing to it and almost zero pointing externally. Sites should return the favor to other quality pieces of content. Use external links to enhance your own content, and you will be providing helpful resources to your audience at the same time.

Anchor text

Anchor text is still important to use strategically. Semantically relevant anchor text helps Google determine what kind of content a link is pointing to.[32] But be sure to use and not abuse it. To give an extreme example, if 100 percent of the anchor text used in a law firm's backlinks is "personal injury lawyer" and their on-page content is also optimized for "personal injury lawyer," their site will likely encounter some sort of penalty. Websites need to diversify their anchor text and the types of content they're optimizing for. If you follow those basic guidelines, you'll be in good shape.

Canonicalization to avoid confusion

When search engines are confused, website rankings will inevitably suffer. Duplicating content on multiple pages of your site is one way to confuse them and dilute ranking potential. Among several tactics, there's ultimately one very simple way to avoid the majority of duplicate content issues: Specify which of the duplicates is the correct one. According to Moz, "whenever content on a site can be found at multiple URLs, it should be canonicalized for search engines."

Canonicalizing URLs typically takes one of the following three forms: redirecting to the correct URL via 301 redirect, using the rel=canonical attribute, or possibly utilizing the parameter handling tool in Google Search Console.

32 https://www.gotchseo.com/anchor-text/

Metrics

It's also essential to use the correct metrics to track and score the value of your efforts. There are three basic metrics to start with:

Page Authority (PA) is a scoring system created by Moz to help predict pagerank based upon links. It combines a host of signals: linking URLs, linking root domains, 301s, 302s, Moz Rank, Moz Trust, anchor text, linking subdomains, new versus old links, domain name, spam score — just to name a few. Moz combines all of this data from their link index and molds the data into findings with some recommendations.

Another frequently used Moz metric is Domain Authority (DA). While PA applies to the page level, DA applies at the root domain level. No subdomains — just root domains. The primary benefit of DA is predicting how well a domain's pages can rank in Google. The higher the DA score, the higher the pages within that domain should rank in the SERP.

The last of the three main Moz metrics is Linking Root Domains. According to Moz, this metric provides, "a count of all the unique root domains with at least one link on them that point to a given page or a site." For example, if Magellan University's website has 300 linking root domains, there are 300 unique domains with at least one link pointing to its website. The catch? This metric combines all links, regardless if they're follow or no-follow. No-follow links don't pass authority, so you'll need to use additional tools to help decipher between the two, such as Majestic or Ahrefs.[33][34]

Optimizing images and videos

To cast as wide a net throughout search engines as possible, optimizing images and videos cannot be overlooked either. And while there isn't quite a one-size-fits-all technique, there are some helpful best practices Google has mentioned to follow.

- **Reduce size to improve load time.** Compress images as much as possible without sacrificing quality.
- **Eliminate unnecessary image resources.** Ask if the image itself actually provides value and the desired impact on the content's overall message.

---

33 https://majestic.com/
34 https://ahrefs.com/

- **Leverage CSS3 effects where possible.** Gradients, shadows and CSS animations can often be utilized to create resolution-independent assets that look sharp at every resolution and zoom level.
- **Use web fonts instead of encoding text in images.** Enable the use of eye-catching typefaces while maintaining the ability to search, select, and resize text.

GIF vs. JPEG vs. PNG image formats

GIF	JPEG	PNG
Only use when animation is required. Poor quality for most standard images.	The most commonly used for photos. Reduces file size significantly while sacrificing very little regarding quality.	Use when high-resolution images or graphics are absolutely necessary.
Transparency	No transparency	Transparency

Figure #40: GIF vs. JPEG vs. PNG image formats

Educate search engines by using descriptive image file names. Since crawlers can't actually view images, you'll have to literally spell out what the image depicts. Use alt text (alternative text) to provide additional information about the image to Google. Alt text is especially important to provide meaning when an image does not render correctly or when someone is visually impaired and needs the use of a screen reader. In fact, alt text is "first and foremost a principle of web accessibility," according to Moz.

Search engines cannot actually view video content, either — they need to be told what's going on. Video optimization all starts with relevant, keyword-rich titles, descriptions or transcripts, and tags. Assigning a category will also help a video show up among related or similar video content. The video's thumbnail and end screen should be intentionally optimized, too. These are the first and last impression viewers have of a piece of video content and can make or break how effective a video is to its intended audience — or if it even gets seen. The end screen is also a perfect opportunity to insert a captivating call-to-action that propels users further on their journey.

Why prioritize local SEO?

Local SEO consists of many different local citation components, which are absolutely vital to the success of any organization hoping to reach to a nearby audience. Whether you are a brick-and-mortar store, a ground campus for a major university or a business that provides a local HVAC service, there are a few local SEO best practices, among many, that should always be accounted for.

First, consistency is key. Whether an organization has one location or dozens, the same concept applies. Ensuring that each location's contact information (Name, Address, and Phone Number) is accurate across all major business directories (and your website, of course) is a simple yet important step that is often overlooked. If a search engine identifies inconsistent contact information across multiple directories, how is it supposed to know which one is right? It won't — nor will a potential customer. This confusion can negatively impact search rankings and local traffic.

To make things more challenging, there are dozens of local citation sites you can optimize, but we suggest focusing on Google My Business, Facebook, Apple Maps, Yelp, Yellow Pages, Bing, and Better Business Bureau for now. There are digital tools to help you manage local citations across sites and ensure everything is consistent. Synup, Moz Local, and Tribe Local are just a few.

Local 3-pack

The holy grail of local search results is commonly referred to as the local 3-pack, consisting of the top 3 map results for a given query. This is the ideal position to be in for any organization that relies on local traffic. Why? To put it simply, that's where most of the clicks happen. According to a recent study conducted by Moz, only 8 percent of searchers choose to load more local results. Meanwhile, 44 percent of people who performed a local search clicked on a local 3-pack listing. Showing up there can be a game-changer for almost any organization.

So, what's the secret sauce for showing up in the local 3-pack? In addition to your citations being accurate and consistent, relevance and distance play a significant role. Relevance comes into play while filling out your Google My Business profile, for example. Choosing what category your business falls under can make a real impact. Generally, the more specific you can be within the broader category, the better. Going too broad with something like "plumber" or "attorney" might not yield the most qualified customers. Try to select specific types of plumbing services or areas of law, if possible.

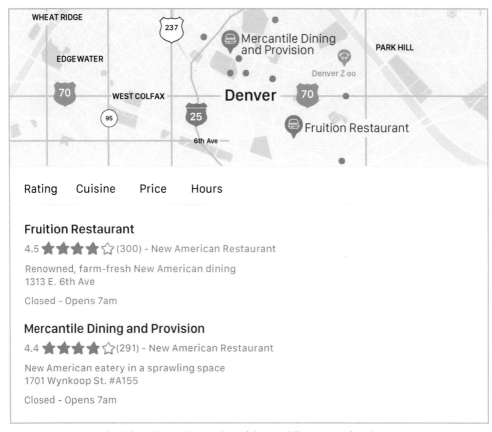

Figure #41: Example of local search results with specific categorization

Obviously, there isn't a whole lot that can be done when it comes to the proximity of a business to a searcher. However, organizations can increase their odds of showing up in the local 3-pack for relevant local searches by building specific location-based pages on their sites and connecting these pages to their Google My Business profiles.

To set your organization apart from your competitors when it comes to local listings, leverage as many aspects of your local citations as you can, including:

- NAP (Name, Address, Phone Number)
- Website
- Reviews
- Images
- Hours

There will always be more ranking factors to consider from a local SEO perspective. But if your business follows these foundational strategies, you'll check the main boxes Google looks for in local search.

SEO needs, you guessed it, *a documented strategy*

In order for websites to earn and maintain their position in the search results with all of the rapid-fire changes Google dishes out, it's important to have an effective SEO strategy in place. Don't put the book down and walk away! An SEO strategy doesn't need to be overly complicated, however.

Your SEO strategy can ultimately consist of three pillars:

Technical SEO

Start with a site audit that focuses on ensuring there are no roadblocks that hinder the search engines from crawling and indexing site content. Even if a site has been audited in the past, it's a good idea to have an audit every year or so to make sure it's still healthy and in good standing with Google. Similar to the way human beings should visit the doctor for their yearly check-up, websites should do the same.

Relevance

Try to make each page of your site as relevant as possible. First, map and assign specific, targeted keywords that offer the best opportunity for traffic to each webpage. Then, optimize all meta elements, such as HTML titles, meta descriptions, H1s and hierarchical headers and other elements that influence search algorithms. Achieve these efforts using a keyword map, page level analysis and ongoing content optimization.

Authority

Authority is primarily determined by off-page factors, such as backlinks. As mentioned earlier, focus on building quality inbound links that increase the search engines' perception that your site is a trusted resource.

Starting with these three foundational pillars, anyone can then break them down further to get more specific and strategic. Assuming a site has been through an audit process and is in good-standing, the next steps are all about maintaining best practices for incremental improvement.

Sophia finds content that
closely relates to her search queries

Back to Sophia's search, "What can you do with an MBA in Marketing?" She starts by clicking on the first listing:

Figure #42: Page Example - TopMBAPros.com

The first result closely matched Sophia's long-tail phrase, but when she tried to click-through to the site, the page took far too long to load. The text populated quickly, but the rest of the page was filled with large images and videos that wouldn't fully download. Being more patient than most, Sophia refreshed the page but noticed the same issue. From there, she bounced off the site, back to the search results with hopes that a different website might load correctly.

What happened?

The website might be authoritative enough to rank highly on page 1 of the SERP, but the individual page Sophia tried to access was clearly not optimized for page-load speed. In the age of instant information, we expect answers to come quickly. If a site won't load in under 3 seconds, 40 percent of people will abandon the site for the next one.[35]

Everyone is all looking for a quick answer. It's why Google began extracting answers from sites to place directly on the search engine result pages as answer boxes and other rich results. Google knows searchers are impatient, and it's doing everything possible to address it.

There could be many variables to explain why TopMBAPros' site was acting sluggish, including:

- Image files were too large and not optimized using .JPEG or .GIF files.
- The landing page was being redirected to a new URL.
- The site was not leveraging browser caching.

Increasing your site speed has the benefit of engaging your audience more effectively, and therefore, Google will help you out in the rankings. How much they'll help you is still up for debate, but we've seen over and over again that positive engagement metrics correlate to fast-loading sites. To reinforce the importance of page-load speed, Amazon determined that a one-second slowdown could cost them $1.6 billion in sales.[36] Users will only get more impatient, and Google is going continue its movement towards an instantaneous internet. Improving your site speed will help you keep up.

"Amazon determined that a one-second slowdown could cost them $1.6 billion in sales."

- Fast Company

35 https://www.thinkwithgoogle.com/intl/en-154/marketing-collections/mobile/mobile-speed-matters/
36 https://www.fastcompany.com/1825005/how-one-second-could-cost-amazon-16-billion-sales

Since Sophia couldn't view the information she wanted from the first result, she clicked the second result. Remember, she's at the beginning stages of her research, learning if this path is even a smart move. Sophia's interested in the types of jobs available if she were to pursue an MBA with a marketing specialization. MBAGrads4Success' article might help narrow down her decision. Unlike the first result, this page loaded very quickly. But, to her disappointment, the information was incredibly thin — a bulleted list of job titles with no further information.

MBA *Grads4Success*

ONLINE	MBA	BLOG	RESOURCES	PROGRAMS	Search...

Types of Jobs After an MBA in Marketing

By: Leo McPherson

- Management Consultant
- Marketing Manager
- Operations Manager
- Director of Marketing

View Recent Blog Posts

Figure #43: Page Example - MBAGrads4success.com

What happened?

Older websites tend to get caught in the middle of old and new strategies — they rank for keyword phrases, but don't create quality content based on user experience. It's clear to Sophia that MBAGrads4Success built this page with the intent of ranking for related keyword phrases but never spent the time to provide quality information to their users. It ranked highly because the website has a strong domain authority and there were many old backlinks built to that page, but we don't expect that page to perform well for very long.

As Google puts more emphasis on user intent and experience, it wouldn't be surprising if this website begins to slide in the rankings if they don't add more information that users find valuable. Unclear of job descriptions, locations, pay scale and benefits, Sophia is forced back — once again — to the search results page.

Sophia is already familiar with Magellan University from a few different touchpoints in her customer journey, and they are the third result. Now, we know what you're thinking: 'Why wouldn't she only click on the result from the company she's most familiar with, like when she bought the school supplies from Target?'

The answer is a testament to how we, as users, use Google search to research information during the customer journey. Remember, the school supply customer journey was fast. Sophia quickly became aware of her needs, considered her options and made a decision to purchase.
But when it comes to enrolling at a university, Sophia makes the responsible choice to slow down on the decision-making process. Makes sense, right?

So, even though she was most familiar with the brand, she opted not to click on the Magellan University result right away. Sophia isn't considering Magellan University (or any college for that matter) to pursue her career advancement yet. She knows the brand but is still researching her options and learning as much as possible before moving forward — and she's doing this, for the most part, subconsciously.

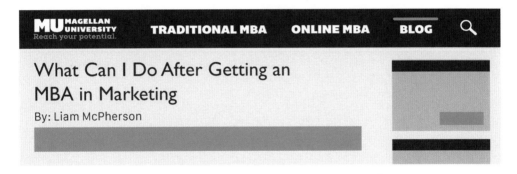

Figure #44: Page Example - MagellanUniversity.com

What happened?

After being disappointed by the first two results, Sophia clicks through to Magellan University's site. This content is stellar. It's visually appealing, it contains valuable information, and it's optimized to promote rankings and click-throughs using SEO best practices. From this single article, Sophia learned about popular careers for MBA grads, including job descriptions, pay scale and geographic areas, and career resources, including alumni groups and networking opportunities for MBA graduates.

Magellan University created a near perfect piece of content for Sophia using most of the best practices we've covered previously in this book. There was just one problem: Once Sophia read the article, there was no next step for her to take, and this would affect her journey dramatically.

Main Takeaways
& Action Steps

1

What strategies from this chapter can you use to earn links that support the way Google ranks content today?

2

What kinds of local searches are relevant to your customers and organization?

3

What can you improve in your SEO strategy: Technical SEO? Relevance? Authority?

CHAPTER V
Sophia abandons one university's funnel and hops on a competitor's

Magellan University's content was very helpful to Sophia. It showcased what type of job she'd like to pursue moving forward in her career — Chief Marketing Officer (CMO). Becoming a CMO for a large brand satisfies most of her professional dreams, and she's motivated to learn more. Like most researchers narrowing their focus, Sophia now wants more details about that specific position.

Unfortunately, after Sophia reads the content from Magellan University, there's no clear next step for her to take in her journey. In other words, when she finished reading content on the page, there was nowhere for her to go on MagellanUniversity.edu that offered content specifically around Chief Marketing Officer careers or resources.

This is a critical lesson in mapping content to the customer's journey. Think about it: From Magellan University's perspective, all the effort to get Sophia this far in her journey was for nothing. Even though they are a large brand with an authoritative website, offered a great piece of content that was optimized for search and pinpointed her interest in a new career path, if Sophia wants to learn more about becoming a CMO, she'll need to continue her research elsewhere. Because of the gap in Magellan's content, Sophia has no choice but to bounce back to the search engine.

How keyword research
and a content audit could have helped

Today, content marketing success boils down to truly understanding your target audience and anticipating their needs and questions at each step of their journey — from awareness to consideration to decision. What factors are Sophia considering next, and what could Magellan have done to provide all the information she needed to stay in their funnel?

Going back to the ideation process outlined in chapter 3, once your core ideas have been established, keyword research can help refine the content strategy by identifying the most commonly used terms and phrases people use when researching a topic. This step is important because it gives content the best chance of being found when people like Sophia refer to search engines to help answer their questions. It's often surprising what phrases people outside of an organization use when it comes to their industry-related questions. Understanding the way your personas use search when they ask questions can make the difference between your content being frequently found and wasting away on page 12 of Google's search results – or not being created at all.

Whether an organization has a new content strategy or has been consistently creating content for years, it cannot possibly know what pieces are missing in relation to its customer's journey without a content audit. If Magellan had audited the content they already had and mapped it to their persona's customer journey, they would have quickly identified that they had missed some of Sophia's needs and, therefore, were missing out on some potentially huge results.

Establishing a strategy
for every step of the journey

Organizations that succeed at digital marketing have at least two things in common: They have a documented strategy, and they publish valuable content on their website that does the heavy lifting for the visitor at each stage of their journey.

In other words, effective content:

- Is thorough and unique
- Speaks to specific audiences or personas
- Always guides visitors toward their next step

In this chapter, we're going to walk through how you can create an online marketing strategy that will ensure you have high quality, appropriate content available, regardless of when a potential customer hits your website.

Don't overthink your strategy

According to the Content Marketing Institute, marketers with a documented strategy are significantly more effective than those who don't have a written strategy. But only about 40 percent of marketers (B2B or B2C) have a documented plan.[37]

> Digital marketing done well requires a company-wide effort. A documented strategy will help you:
>
> - Get everyone in your organization on the same page with your digital marketing goals.
> - Provide guidelines and parameters for your colleagues.
> - Continually remind your teammates of the who, what, where, when and why that fuel your online marketing efforts.

We understand that "strategy" can be a scary word, but don't let it intimidate you. The best digital marketing strategies are simple and easy to understand.[38] Your strategy should be easy to follow — for marketers, executives, product developers, content creators and everyone else at your company. And yet, many organizations get mired in a never-ending process of excessive research and endless interviews when creating their strategy. They put pressure on themselves to come up with a marketing plan that is so groundbreaking, creative and unique that, ultimately, they either stall out or create something so complex it's impossible to execute. But it doesn't have to be like that.

---

37 http://contentmarketinginstitute.com/research/
38 https://insights.newscred.com/content-marketing-is-a-strategic-solution/

Let's be clear:
There is no "original" digital marketing strategy

Companies large and small experiment with all kinds of online marketing tactics, but we all generally have access to the same ingredients:

1. **Paid media strategies.** Online and traditional advertising, often for top-of-funnel, awareness-stage content.
2. **Owned media strategies.** The content and overall user experience you provide on your website, app and e-publications, often for mid-funnel, consideration-stage content.
3. **Earned media.** The good (and bad) things people say or share about you on social media, review sites and elsewhere, often for lower-funnel, decision-stage content.

Paid media is arguably the easiest and most expensive strategy to employ. Earned media is the hardest (it's called "earned" for a reason), but it's technically the cheapest.

The middle strategy — owned media — can be a catalyst for success in all areas of online marketing because you will be building and communicating directly with your own audience. But if you ignore your owned channels, such as your website, then it will be practically impossible for you to be effective with your advertising, social media and other digital efforts because you'll be directing your prospects to a mediocre experience at best.

In the end, your marketing strategy will likely combine elements of paid, owned and earned ingredients, following strategic best practices that we'll cover in this chapter.

Pick the strategies that make the most sense for:

• Your business
• The resources you have available
• And, most importantly, your customers

Trust us. You'll learn infinitely more by executing a simple, documented strategy than you will by exhaustively researching your audiences and your industry for months on end. Research and preparation are important, but you've got to press the launch button at some point.

Assumptions and educated guesses can't compete with real-world data. Once you start publishing content, you'll be able to measure the performance of your website's new assets, and those learnings should help you refine your strategy. A truly valuable digital marketing strategy will evolve over time based on the analytics you collect from your efforts.

Think about strategy with an "agile" mindset that repeats continuously:[39]

- Test
- Learn
- Iterate

Documenting your digital strategy

The components of even a "bare bones" digital marketing strategy should include answers to the following seven questions:

1. Business Goals:
Why are we doing this?

What is the end goal for your organization's digital efforts? These goals will be your ongoing compass, so it's best if your they're rooted in very specific business objectives. Think business with a capital B and remember: If you have more than three priorities, you have none. So pick one, two or — at most — three objectives that are important to your organization. A lack of focus will lead to a lack of results.

Paint a picture of your ideal future state, and then work backward: How will your one, two or three business objectives help you achieve those goals, and how can you measure them digitally? Here are some examples:

---

39 http://www.verticalmeasures.com/content-strategy/agile-content-marketing-strategies-102016/

Business Objective	Ideal Future State (soft goal)	KPI (hard goal)
Sales / Retention	We want so much revenue that we can go public in 5 years.	# customers, profitability
Leads	We want to build our owned audience by having the biggest e-mail newsletter in our industry.	"Request Information" forms completed, content downloads, email subscribers, consultations scheduled
Brand Awareness	We want to be mentioned when people ask, "Who are the 3 leading providers in this industry?"	Website traffic, social shares, content placed on other sites, more branded searches.
Educate our Audience / Thought Leadership	We want to speak at industry-leading conferences.	Average session duration, return website visitors, inbound links, webinar sign-ups
Audience Engagement	We want our groups and social channels to refer customers.	Average time on page, bounce rate, social mentions, shares and referrals

Figure #45: Establishing business goals

2. Audience Needs: Who are we targeting?

This is perhaps the most important piece of the strategy puzzle. Why? Because if you want to build your own audience to gain a competitive advantage, then you need to know precisely who you are targeting and how you can help them.

Once you understand the questions and pain points your audience has, you begin to understand what information they might search for online. Then, you can produce focused content assets for each persona, at each step of their customer journey.

This kind of focused, helpful content stands a far better chance at performing well online and ranking in search engines than sweeping, generic pieces of content. If you don't create personas and work toward educating and helping your specific audiences, you may end up trying to be all things to all people with your content. And, ultimately, that will attract no one.

Another benefit of creating narrow content pieces for specific personas is that it will give you a longer runway of content ideas.[40] More ideas means you can publish consistently for that much longer. If you work for a cruise company, you could write a content piece about your latest destination that's targeted toward retired grandparents, and then write a second piece about the same destination that targets working executives. And so on.

You likely have a good idea of how many "types" of customers you have: Two? Five? Seven? If we plot out their characteristics, goals and pain points, and then "personify" them, it gives your team of writers and editors a clear picture of who you're actually writing the content for. Here are some examples of potential personas for Magellan University:

Frank Poles

Age: 35 years old   Education: Some college

Occupation: Marketing Freelance   Income: $40,000

Hobbies: Teaching local swimming classes, running half marathons

Personality: Friendly, limited attention span

Motivations: Start a career at a Fortune 1000 company

Influencers: Sports figures

Online/Social Media Habits: Checks mobile phone constantly; spends a lot of time on YouTube

Pain Points/Needs: He is tired of freelancing and wants more stability. He believes finishing school will help him, but he isn't sure which approach he should take.

Content Formats: Watches instructional videos; avoids long-form content

Figure #46a: Strategically building audiences - Frank Poles Persona

Sophia West

Age: 30 years old   Education: Bachelor's, marketing

Occupation: Brand Marketing Specialist   Income: $50,000

Hobbies: Reading, traveling, activities with kids

Personality: Driven, Curious, a voracious reader

Motivations: Provide for her family

Pain Points/Needs: Wants to learn about how she can advance in her career, to be more fulfilled

Influencers: Leading thinkers in business and marketing

Online/Social Media Habits: Researches trends on LinkedIn

Content Formats: Essays, infographics, videos, opinion pieces

Figure #46b: Strategically building audiences - Sophia West Persona

You may need to use a bit of a broad brush here. The key is not to paint so broadly that you have only one persona. You want to write and publish content that speaks directly to your different personas. It's the difference between having a one-on-one conversation and lecturing in front of a huge, disengaged audience.

3. Current State Analysis:
What's happening in your online space?

Now that you have documented your organization's goals and understand your audience, it's time to examine what you and your competitors are currently doing with online marketing.

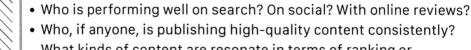

- Who is performing well on search? On social? With online reviews?
- Who, if anyone, is publishing high-quality content consistently? What kinds of content are resonate in terms of ranking or engagement?

- Whose social media profiles are growing or inspiring interaction? How are they doing this?
- Do you or your competitors have sophisticated, automated email workflows that address the customer journey?

Many pitfalls can exist when you start this exercise. Beyond the potentially massive scope, you may have perceived competitors who actually do not compete with you online for similar keyword phrases. Second, seeing what your competitors are publishing on their websites may dissuade you into thinking, 'If they're already publishing about these topics, there's nothing else for us to write about.'

But remember what we said before: There's always room to improve.

Can your organization:

- Address customer journey gaps in the awareness, consideration, decision or advocacy stage?
- Offer content, expertise or an angle that your competitors can't?
- Find online platforms where your competitors are struggling or absent?
- Provide a more seamless user experience through the customer journey?
- Be more specific, more helpful, more relevant or more creative with your content?

4. Strategic Initiatives:
What specific tactics will we employ?

Take the knowledge gained from your current-state analysis, and develop specific tactics to achieve your business goals and meet your audience's needs. These tactics will become your "strategic initiatives." They could be related to content creation, lead generation, SEO, online promotion and more, depending on your goals and what your audience wants.

Examples of strategic initiatives could include:

- Build the first all-encompassing resource center for our industry to drive thought leadership.
- Publish online business listings for all our locations to improve local SEO.
- Build a database of email addresses we can market to when we launch new products.

Your initiatives should clearly tie back to your business goals. Whenever possible:

- Apply your efforts to strategic initiatives that allow you to be efficient.
- Choose "pressure points" that your organization can take advantage of.
- Test and measure your tactics and initiatives for a few months. What did you learn? What should you change?

5. Content Roadmap and Ideation: What is our Content Plan?

Content will likely be one of the core elements to your digital marketing strategy.

Formulate a content roadmap that outlines:

- Topics you have expertise in.
- Channels where you will publish your content.
- Formats that your audience will appreciate.

Remember, you're building on all the previous elements from this chapter, so each piece of content should map back to a business goal, persona and strategic initiative.

First, think about what content you can feasibly create with the resources you have. We almost always recommend rooting your strategy in the production of articles and blog posts because text is how Google and other search engines can best understand, crawl and rank your website.

But content consumption habits are changing, and attention spans continue to decline. While you may create much of the text for SEO purposes, your content has to keep your audience engaged, too.

Beyond blogs and web copy, think about other types of content:
- Videos
- eBooks
- Infographics
- Quizzes
- Checklists
- Reviews and comparisons

Where will you publish all this content? Your website is your "home base" for content — after all, you want to get as much SEO value as possible. For that reason, your content should usually live on your primary domain (i.e. MagellanUniversity.edu/blog), rather than on a subdomain (i.e. blog. MagellanUniversity.edu) to concentrate the SEO value on one site.

Beyond your primary domain, your content roadmap should outline other places you need to publish or promote your content to support your digital strategy.

Ask yourself:
- Where do our personas get their information online? Can we establish a presence there?
- Which social media channels do we have? Which do our personas use?
- Are there any third-party, partner or industry sites that can help us distribute our content?
- Are there forums and discussion groups (i.e. LinkedIn, Quora) where we should become active?
- What messaging should we use in our ad campaigns and on our landing pages?
- What kind of information do our personas want to receive in our email newsletter?

Digital marketing is all about consistency. Google has a bias for fresh content, and it has a bias for disciplined publishers of that content.[41] Whatever your cadence is (four times per month or dozens of times per month), stick to that rhythm by using a content calendar, as mentioned previously. Create it. Follow it. Love it.

Delegate the tasks and content pieces in your content calendar to relevant teams, and hold your teams accountable to the agreed upon topics, formats, target audiences and due dates.

6. Data:
How will we continuously measure success?

This question should clearly tie back to your answers from Question 1 and Question 4. Assign a KPI to each strategic initiative, and monitor these KPIs at least monthly. Doing so will trigger our test-learn-iterate philosophy — you'll see what's working, what's not and how you can pivot or evolve to do even better. Strategy is never "one and done." You should always go back and refine your strategy based on performance, industry trends and changing organizational goals.

You can track many KPIs within your web analytics program. Example KPIs include:

- Number of leads collected from form fills each month.
- Percent reduction in bounce rate from your website.
- Percent increase of email as a source of website traffic.

7. Governance:
Who will help execute our strategy?

You won't get far into implementing your digital marketing strategy or measuring your efforts if you don't have the commitment of your teams. To have success, it's absolutely critical to get your people on board with your strategy and make sure they know what will be expected of them.[42]

---

41 https://moz.com/blog/google-fresh-factor-new
42 http://contentmarketinginstitute.com/2016/12/company-involved-content-marketing/

For your teammates who are interested and able to pitch in, it should be made part of their job description that they contribute to online marketing — this isn't optional. Half-hearted commitments will yield delayed or even poor online marketing results. So, who should help with execution, and who should make the final calls on certain decisions?

Strategists

- A small team of decision makers should ensure everyone else involved adheres to the strategic initiatives.

Marketers

- Marketers study which tactics (paid, social, organic, promotion) have the most impact toward your business objectives so you can adjust accordingly.

Sales

- Sales teams should have a sense of what customers want and where the industry is going, which you can use for ideation.

Subject matter experts (SMEs)

- SMEs can inform and even help produce your most authoritative content.

Anyone customer-facing

- These people know what's plaguing prospects and the content you need to create to overcome objections.

Creatives

- Writers, designers, videographers, editors and other creators produce your quality copy, graphics, videos and more.

Tech staff

- You need programmers, web editors and other IT support to craft digital experiences that work for your audience.

Business partners or suppliers

- Not all contributors have to be internal. Do you have clients, partners, vendors or freelancers who could contribute to your online strategy?

Aligning your strategy
with the customer journey

Let's return to Question 2 above ("Who is our audience?") and go into greater detail. Part of knowing who your personas are is knowing how they find your product or service and what ultimately impacts their decision whether to do business with you or not.

We often picture the customer journey as a funnel, which essentially represents a series of milestones in your potential customer's research process. You need to understand these milestones to have a sound digital strategy. Most personas will go through three broad stages in their decision-making process.

Imagine you are a solar panel company targeting a homeowner in their mid-30s:

Customer Journey Stage	What the Persona is Doing	Real Life Example	Your Business Goals
Awareness	Your persona has identified a problem they want to solve or becomes exposed to your product, service or idea.	Homeowner wants to lower his monthly utility bills. Is also motivated to "go green."	• Brand exposure • Website traffic
Consideration	They research possible solutions to their problem.	Homeowner learns he has many appealing options: purchase updated appliances, conserve energy, purchase or lease solar panels.	• Engagement (i.e. time on site)
Decision	They compare vendors who provide that specific solution. They decide on a particular solution.	Homeowner decides to purchase a solar panel system.	• Conversions

Figure #47: Aligning your strategy with the customer journey

The fundamental flaw in the marketing funnel is the concept that potential customers are going to find you at the beginning of their research, stay on your website, stay some more, download your eBook, and purchase – all under your marketing umbrella. How could they possibly get diverted or stray from your funnel with all the amazing content you have on your site? This is an obsolete idea in our online world, with multitudes of news sites, review sites, competitor websites, social channels, paid ads and more. People are going to jump around in a plethora of paths, and we need to be ready to welcome them whenever they stumble upon our content.

Now, imagine that you and a neighboring home just learned you'll both be hosting outdoor dinner parties. Everyone in the neighborhood is invited, but you don't know who is coming to which house or when. How do you prepare? Here are two possible approaches:

Washington Household	Adams Household
Appetizers • Chips and salsa • Fruit • Shrimp cocktail	• Cheese pizza • Veggie pizza • Hawaiian pizza
Entrées • Burgers and fries • Pork and veggie skewers • Vegetarian lasagna	
Desserts • New York cheesecake • Key lime pie	

Figure #48: Block party essentials

The neighbors begin showing up randomly at each house on our big party day. What happens? Of course, the Washington household is better prepared for all types of visitors.

They have food for:

- Grazers
- All-you-can-eaters
- Vegetarians
- Gluten-free and lactose-intolerant folks
- People who got bored at the Adams' party

Your neighborhood friends (potential customers) could stop by your house (your website) at the beginning of the day, the end or anywhere in between. If you are prepared with appetizers, entrées and desserts, you have a much better chance at keeping them at your party. The problem with the Adams household — and why Magellan University lost Sophia — is that there just isn't enough substance at the party to keep people there. They also aren't offering visitors a logical next step. After pizza, then what?

As marketers, we must politely nudge our website visitors toward possible next steps, and there should always be a next step — preferably in the form of an obvious, clickable button:

- Read a related blog post
- Find out more about a product
- Subscribe to our newsletter
- Read a testimonial
- Download an eBook
- Add to cart

How to create a customer journey map

You don't want to end up like Magellan University, or some poor soul who hosted a block party that everyone left after five minutes. How do you avoid that? First, don't offer Hawaiian pizza — it's gross. Second, take the "funnel" concept to the next level.

Imagine once again you are a solar panel company. Here's a sketched-out customer journey map for two of your personas:

Customer Journey Stage	Content Ideas for Persona #1 (homeowner motivated by cost savings)	Content Ideas for Persona #2 (homeowner motivated by "going green")
Awareness	**Blog Posts:** • 4 Things You Didn't Know that are Raising Your Utility Bill • How to Read Your Utility Bill: Is It Calculated Correctly?	**Blog Posts:** • Top 10 Ways To Make Your House "Green" • How to Reduce Your Carbon Footprint in San Diego
Consideration	**Video:** • How to Properly Seal Your Windows **Blog Post:** • Top 7 California Tax Credit Options For Homeowners	**Video:** • How to Replace your Aging Air Conditioner **Infographic:** • Best U.S. Cities for Generating Your Own Solar Power
Decision	**Blog Post:** • Solar-Riffic Inc. vs. Solar-tastic LLC — Installation and Price Differences **eBook:** • Why Purchasing Solar Panels Saves More Money than Leasing	**Blog Post:** • Top 20 Questions to Ask Your Solar Contractor **eBook:** • Your Guide to the Most Environmentally Friendly Solar Installers in Southern California

Figure #49: Sample content idea map

Now you have a customer-focused content plan starting to take shape. If you produce content for all of the stages and personas in the table above, you'll be able to meet your customers' various needs at different stages of their journey and research process.

Mapping your content ideas to the customer journey is just a first step, but it's a big one that will get you on the right path. As you can imagine, customer journey maps can get much more sophisticated than our example. You might have 10 personas with five stages each, and within each square of your grid, you could have many different content ideas.

When you're creating these maps, blank squares are your content gaps. If you have content gaps, you risk that persona falling out of touch with you and your content. It's critical to identify your various personas, their stages and their pain points, and then create content for every step of their journeys. If you don't, your competitors will no doubt fill those content gaps.

Don't be like Magellan University — avoid making these mistakes:

- Relying too heavily on your reputation alone
- Publishing broad content that speaks to too wide an audience
- Not doing the heavy lifting for readers and not guiding them step-by-step

Last but not least, for every piece of content — blog post, email or otherwise — use a call-to-action to explicitly tell your readers what to do next, or at least politely guide them to their best option(s). You've spent a lot of time and effort getting people to land on your website. Don't leave them wondering, "Now what?"

Main Takeaways
& Action Steps

1

What are 2-3 personas that make sense for your business?
What do you know about them?

2

Of the strategic questions outlined in this chapter, which
ones do you need to explore further?

3

What content gaps can you identify in your existing
content based on your customers' journeys?

CHAPTER VI
Sophia continues her journey with Coronado University

Sophia is back at the office. She had to pause her research for several weeks to focus on other priorities. A client failed to bite on an RFP that took weeks to create, and Stonecreek Digital was all hands on deck to try and recover the lost revenue. It's now October, her kids are in school and the holiday season is ramping up.

Stonecreek Digital hosts Friday Dog Days, so Sophia's bringing her pitbull, Sugar, into the office. Dog days are a favorite around the office, slowing down the chaos of every day with cold noses, wet kisses and some unconditional love. But for Sophia, having Sugar around at work doesn't offer the same fulfillment as it used to. She's not unhappy at work, but she feels certain that something is missing in her professional life.

Between meetings, Sophia picks up where she left off on her customer journey. After reaching a dead end with Magellan University, she's determined to find the information she needs to go back to school and advance her career. Stonecreek Digital (and their dog days) are familiar to Sophia, but like many of us, she knows that to achieve greatness, you must become comfortable with being uncomfortable. Sophia is ready to get out of her comfort zone and find a way to achieve her career goals. Relying on Google search again, she picks up where she left off. "How to be a chief marketing officer" is her first entry in the search bar.

The results showcase the usual suspects — MBA lead generation sites, Magellan University and a few other big-name brands. But at lucky position 7 on page one of the SERPs, a new result appears and grabs Sophia's attention.

Coronado University is a smaller school located in southern California, about 45 minutes from Sophia's home. While it doesn't have the marketing budget that Magellan University does, Coronado University has spent a great amount of time working on their digital marketing strategy to get the most ROI from their efforts. The university understands organic search best practices — and perhaps more importantly — they understand and cater to Sophia's customer journey.

The meta description of their search result is optimized to entice the most click-throughs from users. While not considered a ranking factor for Google, meta descriptions are crucial to get more traffic to any website. If a description sets the wrong expectation, confuses readers or doesn't excite them enough, the content has little chance to perform optimally.

The content for the Coronado University page, "How to be a Successful CMO," is high-quality and 10 times better than most of what Sophia had read a few weeks ago when she started her research. There was actually similar information in the Magellan University article, but this time, the user experience was exponentially better. From this page, she learned more about the real role and responsibilities of a chief marketing officer and how to thrive in that position. In the back of her mind, Sophia decided: Magellan University might show up in her search results again, but Coronado University would be her go-to resource from now on. Coronado University had content for Sophia at every stage of her journey, and they quickly picked up where the competition left off.

After reading the article from Coronado University, Sophia is energized to learn more and is drawn to a call-to-action (CTA) for a quiz about becoming a CMO at the end of the piece.

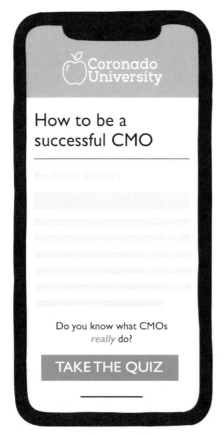

The power of CTAs

The CTA invites Sophia to take a quiz and get on the right path toward advancing her career. Her intentions are pretty innocent at this point. She thinks the quiz will be a fun way to kill some time before her next meeting, and the role of CMO has held her interest for quite some time. Her expectations for the assessment are fairly low, but at the same time, she holds hope that the results will give her some clarity to help follow through with her customer journey and decide how to advance her career.

Figure #50: Coronado University Quiz CTA

Coronado University uses the
Hub & Spoke model

There are a few variations of the Hub & Spoke model. Some consider your entire website the "hub." While this model can be quite successful, we take the Hub & Spoke model a little deeper.

In our model, you research, produce and publish a main piece of content that customers really want, which becomes the hub. Then, you create many spokes that relate back to that significant piece of content to support, promote and drive more and more traffic to it.

The hub is a high-value piece of content like a case study, eBook, extensive infographic, video or another asset that is rich enough to entice a user to trade something for it, like their contact information. The hub is published first, and the spokes are published continuously for several months afterward (sometimes longer depending on the focus and the nature of the piece) in different formats and different channels that can engage people at different stages of their journey.

The spokes are published to drive traffic to the hub, while the hub helps drive conversions, whether they are email sign-ups, requests for more info, sales or another action that matters to your organization. Without a hub, the spokes would be miscellaneous pieces and types of content that may not be tied to any specific marketing goals or conversion strategy. Hubs and spokes are dependent on each other. They need to be done in tandem because without spoke content promoting and distributing, the hub may not get enough traffic to be successful.

In the case of Coronado University, their quiz is a hub, and Sophia found it though a spoke that piqued her interested from her stage of the customer journey — the article about how to be a successful CMO.

Think of the Hub & Spoke model as an image or illustration. The hub is located at the center, and the spokes all connect back to it like a wagon wheel. As the wheel rolls forward, it gains traction and moves traffic along the spokes directly to the hub. In distributed computing, it's known as a star network. In nature, it's called a spider web.

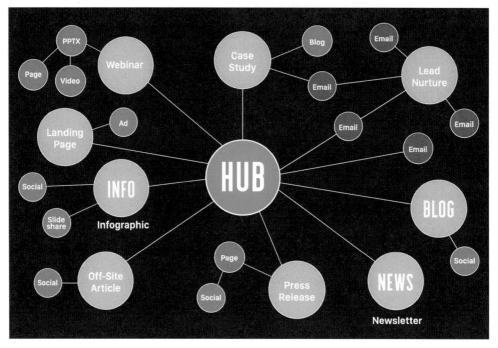

Figure #51: Vertical Measures' Hub & Spoke Model

Not to be confused with a blog section of a website, a hub part in the model we're describing is a specific piece of content like a user guide, a buying guide, a how-to guide, a white paper, a case study, a buyer's comparison guide, a sophisticated, animated infographic, a high-level video or webinar or some other valuable resource. The commonality of these content pieces is their depth and breadth. The content is rich and high-quality. It's a piece of content that a user would be happy to trade their email address or other personal information to access. In most cases, the hub content should be placed behind a lead capture form. By capturing an email address, marketers can start to lead-nurture, developing a deeper relationship with this new contact to potentially move them along in their customer journey.

> **"96% of visitors who come to your site are not ready to buy — but they may be willing to trade contact information for valuable content."**
>
> - Marketo

Hub Examples

eBook

An eBook is a rich, long-format digital book that includes text, images, graphs, pull quotes, bulleted lists, numbered lists, embedded video and other content elements designed to break up the text for users that like to skim and quickly find the information they are looking for. The eBook should be long enough and interesting enough for users to be willing to trade information for the download. The richness of an eBook should allow you to capture more than just an email address. The more focused and valuable the hub, the more data points you should be able to collect from the user. For example, in addition to an email address, you might also request company name, title within the company, size of the organization, annual revenue and other information that's relevant to your sales efforts.

Webinar

Webinars are web-based seminars, live presentations where users remotely engage in the presentation from their desktops. These are fantastic ways to bring together customers from anywhere on the planet. The limitations on participation are only a matter of user access to the internet at the time your webinar takes place (or afterward, if you record it). To manage connectivity and presentation, you can use a webinar service like GoToMeeting, ON24, Webex or another hosting platform.

Figure #52: Vertical Measures webinar example

Usually, webinar presentations are displayed using PowerPoint, but anything that you can share on your computer monitor can be shown on a webinar. Because webinars are interactive, anyone who has joined the webinar can interact with questions or even co-host the presentation. When we host webinars, we also record them and post the recording to our site so people who missed them can find it later.[43]

In essence, webinars are videos, but because of their educational content, it's more common for people to get over their short video threshold and engage with webinars for up to an hour. A prerecorded webinar is a great example of hub content. As you've already created it from a live session, the whole hub is actually repurposed. Put this behind a lead capture form, and you've got a hub you can start driving traffic to.

Video

There are a number of video variations that can be used as hubs. For example: an interview with an executive or thought leader that answers some of the most-commonly-asked questions about their position or industry, or a product or service walk-through that explains in great detail what a potential customer can expect from your company (also called an explainer video). We'll explain how to use video in-depth in chapter 12.

Podcast

The popular term "podcast" (as opposed to "webcast") came about with the invention of the iPod, which is why podcasts are often associated with audio syndication. But technology for mobile devices is constantly evolving, and today's multimedia devices can handle video without any trouble. That wasn't the case when podcasts were first introduced.

Today, podcasts have evolved with device technology and now often include video versions, as well. So now, you can double-down on the recordings and distribute videos you produce from podcasting, too. Since today's podcasts can be audio or video, they make for versatile content that can be effortlessly distributed to organic visitors in the format they prefer.

---

43 http://www.verticalmeasures.com/webinars/

Podcast content is portable so it's a great way to get users to trade personal info for content, even when they're on the go. You should also consider transcribing your podcasts so when the user downloads the audio file, they can also scan the transcript. Publishing podcasts is a great way to build an owned audience over time. A best practice is to publish your podcasts on a regular schedule so users always know when to tune in.

Calculators

Calculators[44] act as great hubs that can showcase the benefits of your product or service accurately so users can justify selecting you. Create interactive calculators so users can actively input relevant information, and then ask for their email address to unlock their results. Users that interact with calculators are generally further along in their customer journey, so make sure to include calls-to-action and contact information on results pages to help move potential customers closer to a decision.

CRO Calculator

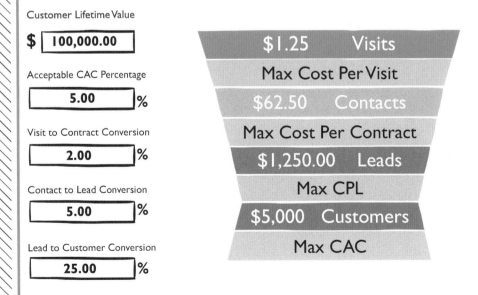

Figure #53: Vertical Measures' CRO Calculator

Spokes

Spokes can be a series of blog posts related to a hub, a press release announcing the hub, tweets, Facebook posts, infographics, videos, native advertising, paid promotions, webinars relating back to the guide or other rich pieces of content that include a link or call-to-action to download the hub content. Often, we'll actually take a portion of our hub content, reformat it and repurpose it to make the most out of the time and resources we invested in the project.

Spoke content reaches back to revive its hub and extends forward to promote and distribute the content. You can continually revive your hub content because of its high value. Generally, hubs are "evergreen" and only need to be refreshed from time to time to stay relevant.

Here is a list of spoke content examples. What would you add to it?

- A series of blog posts
- A series of interviews or videos
- A SlideShare presentation
- A motion graphics video
- An infographic
- A series of graphics pulled from the infographic and shared on social
- Syndicated articles
- Guest post(s) on other sites
- A series of Facebook posts
- A series of tweets
- References to the hub in an email series

How to deploy the Hub & Spoke model

To be successful with our Hub & Spoke model, you must consider a number of things before creating the interconnected content.

Goal of the project

Begin with the end in mind. What is the goal or outcome you want to achieve by using this model? Do you want to move users further along in your customer journey? Do you want to convert them to a customer? Do you just want to capture their email address and get permission to email them in order to build a relationship? These questions help you determine what to ask for in exchange for access to the hub.

Determine hub topics

The next step is to determine the topic or theme of your hub. What are you going to write about and why? Consider the following as you brainstorm ideas on what to produce:

- Are people searching for this information?
- Would people or other sites link to this piece of content?
- Would this topic be shareable on social media?
- Could you use this asset in outreach efforts?
- Could you take elements from the hub and repurpose it in other channels?
- Does it provide enough value for a user to trade information for it?
- Do you have the resources or access to resources that can help you create it?

Hub format

Once you determine the topic, decide on the format of the hub. Will it be an eBook? A complex infographic? An interactive quiz like the one Sophia discovered? Often, the topic or theme will lead you to the best format for the content. The goal and persona you're targeting will also have a strong influence on what format you should use. You'll also want to decide where the hubs will be published (usually on a dedicated landing page on your website).

Spoke format

Once you've decided on the hub format, it's time to consider the format and frequency of the spoke content. As you consider the publishing channels you'll use, think about organic and paid distribution. By now, you should know who your audience is and where they hang out online. These are the places you will want to publish your spokes.

Most of the spokes you'll create and publish will reside on your own website, like the hub. By publishing most of the content on your own site, you'll be increasing your keyword footprint and the opportunity to rank for more keywords in the search engines. You'll also be building related pages on your site that can point links back to the hub. These thematic pages will help you rank for semantically related keywords that support the hub content and your overall authority on the topic. As you publish these spokes on your site, cross-link to other internal pages and to the hub landing page to boost their impact.

If you've done a good job of planning your hubs and spokes, you should have graphics, quotes, images and other high-quality content that you can parse from the hub itself. Repurpose this content on your business' social pages. Repurposing content creates efficiencies in both time and cost. The graphics and images you repurpose will also help brand the hub and keep everything looking consistent across all channels. If you share your site content on Facebook, implement Facebook Open Graph on your website. This tool provide easy control over the look and feel of information that is shared from a site on Facebook. If you use WordPress, adding the tool takes just a simple plugin.

How we use Hub & Spoke

The following diagram is an example of how we do Hub & Spoke at Vertical Measures. First, we launch a big piece of content and feature it on our home page. Then, we spoke the heck out of it for 90 days – and in the case of this book, even longer. We treat our hub content like a product or brand launch.

It's kind of a big deal.

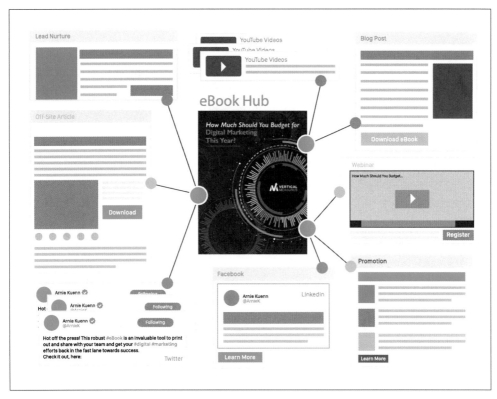

Figure #54: Hub & Spoke Model in action

The Vertical Measures' Budget eBook provides useful tools to help marketing teams set and plan their next marketing budget for the year.[45] To promote it, we sent emails, distributed a press release, scheduled social messages and more. Every few months, we launch another piece of hub content and do the same thing — rinse and repeat. We publish hub content about once per quarter.

Effectively using the Hub & Spoke model is not easy, and it can take considerable resources to deploy. If you've just started down the path of content marketing, don't feel like you have to jump right into this model. Learn the basics first. Get your production resources in place until you have a repeatable, easy-to-follow process. Once you have the fundamentals in place and you've proven you can create quality content within your deadlines, start planning and producing this kind of robust hub content regularly. If you want to start now, engage a trusted content marketing partner to help get rich, high-quality content live sooner.

---

45 http://vert.ms/budget-ebook

Creating effective calls-to-action

As we've mentioned, calls-to-action (CTAs) help move users from page to page on your website. Creating strong CTAs can help direct prospects to the next step in your customer journey. By consistently adding CTAs to your content, you always let the prospect know what to do next. Often, we assume people will know what to do next, but users don't usually want to think that hard. Consider a page with lots of copy on it that you arrived at from a paid ad. Once we landed here we weren't sure what to do. This business paid for you to land here but didn't lead you through the content to the next click.

Figure #55: Creating effective calls-to-action

Start your call-to-action with a strong action verb like buy, shop, learn, download, order — you get the idea. Let users know what they're going to get if they click. Once you've determined the action you want them to take, add context that lets the audience know the benefit of clicking, the "What's in it for me?" (WIIFM). You'll have better results when users know why they should click. Will they save money, lose weight, get more free time, see faster results?

While we're talking acronyms, here's another: FOMO, or fear of missing out. FOMO CTAs are intended to get the prospect to act quickly, out of a sense of urgency or scarcity.

A few FOMO ideas include:
- Sale ends Saturday   • Limited supply   • Only 5 left in stock

How do you determine the right call to action? A/B testing is a good way to learn what's working. Doing an A/B split test will let you know what words or phrases get the most clicks. If you have enough traffic, you can learn quickly, iterate and make adjustments. Here are some sample CTAs to get you thinking — what would you add?

- Add to cart
- Start your 14-day free trial now
- Reserve your seat
- Sign up now — it's free!
- Save 50% today only!
- Subscribe for the inside scoop
- Join the club
- Request more info

Look at the following six-month content marketing plan. It includes hub and spoke content. What do you like about it? What tweaks would you make? What content and formats would you add to it?

A sample
Hub & Spoke schedule

Month One

- Create one (1) **eBook** hub
- Create eight (8) **blog post** spokes
- Create (1) **press release** for eBook
- Promote eBook in email
- Promote eBook in social media channels*
- Share blog posts on social media channels

Month Two

- Create five (5) **blog posts**
- Create one (1) **guest blog post** and link back to eBook
- Create three (3) **graphics** to support eBook
- Promote eBook in social media channels*
- Promote blog content in social media channels*
- Share graphics on social media channels

*organic and paid

Month Three

- Create five (5) **blog posts**
- Create one (1) **case study** to support eBook
- Create one (1) **press release** for case study

- Promote case study in social media channels*
- Promote blog posts in social media channels*

Month Four

- Create five (5) **blog posts**
- Create one (1) **guest blog post** and link back to eBook
- Create one (1) **slide deck** on SlideShare.net about the eBook

- Promote eBook in social media channels*
- Promote blog content in social media channels*
- Promote webinar based on SlideShare in social channels* and email

Month Five

- Create six (6) **blog posts**
- Create one (1) **guest blog post** and link back to case study
- Create one (1) **infographic**

- Promote infographic in social media channels*
- Share blog content in social media channels
- Promote recording of webinar on social media channels*

Month Six

- Create one (1) new **eBook**
- One (1) **press release** for infographic created and published month 5
- Create six (6) **blog posts**
- Create one (1) **guest blog post** and link back to case study

- Promote new ebook in social channels* and email – rinse and repeat!

*organic and paid

Figure #56: Sample Hub & Spoke schedule

To gate, or not to gate?

To gate, or not to gate: that is the question. It's a common dilemma for marketers today. Do the pros of gating premium content outweigh the cons of asking for personal information from your visitors? In this section, we'll offer an answer to this great gate debate and provide some best practices to implement your own gated content to drive more traffic, leads and revenue for your business.

What is gated content?

Gated content is any media that's placed behind a lead capture form. In other words, a user must provide personal information in order to access the content — typically an email address, phone number or answer to a low-friction question. For example, Coronado University uses a "gate" or lead capture form in front of several content marketing resources:

Figure #57: Coronado University Sample Resource Page Example

The majority of Coronado University's gated content is 10x, premium content that provides exceptional value based on their audience's needs. By providing a valuable resource, this gated content allows the school to gather qualified leads by asking for more information about their readers, including their name, email address, job title and how soon they want to go back to school.

While a few publishers limit access to everyday content by requiring a subscription or newsletter sign-up (we're looking at you, Adweek), most publishers only gate premium content like eBooks and other forms of rich, in-depth content.[46]

---

46 https://moz.com/blog/how-to-create-10x-content-whiteboard-friday

Gated
Content Examples

- Contests
- Templates
- Tools
- Checklists
- eBooks

- Guides
- White Papers
- Webinars
- Training videos

Non-Gated
Content Examples

- Articles/Blog Posts
- Curated Content
- Infographics
- Lists
- Press Releases

- Visuals (images, videos, GIFs)
- Snippets (from 10x content or hubs)
- Testimonials

Figure #58: Gated and non-gated content examples

Why use gated content vs. non-gated content?

Marketers can't seem to agree on whether to use gated or non-gated content — for good reason. There are trusted experts and industry leaders on both sides of the debate. On one side, some marketers believe that the pros of gaining qualified leads outweigh the con of turning away potential visitors. Others claim that by asking for personal information, you'll lose potential readers, SEO value and link opportunities.

This debate can actually be narrowed down to a single question: Are you interested in generating page views or qualified leads?

The gated content debate

"Pro-gaters" will most likely agree with the philosophy of Lola.com CEO, Mike Volpe:[47]

If I can get 100,000 people to see that page and I can get 28,000 people to fill it out, 28,000 contacts may be more valuable than even 50,000 people seeing the content.

Figure #59: Pro-gater's position (Source: Mike Volpe)

47 http://cdn2.hubspot.net/hub/53/blog/docs/ebooks/debate%20ebook%20final.pdf

"Anti-gaters" might lean more toward David Meerman Scott's viewpoint:

A lot of people will see the form and say, 'Forget it. I don't want to fill out the form.' The vast majority of people are unwilling to share a piece of content that has a form in front of it. A lot fewer people will blog and tweet something that has a form on it.

Figure #60: Anti-gater's position (Source: David Meerman Scott)

Let's look at both arguments.

Imagine that you're really interested in learning how to make smarter marketing budgets. As you scroll through your Twitter feed, you notice that Arnie Kuenn shared a post about how much to budget for digital marketing this year.

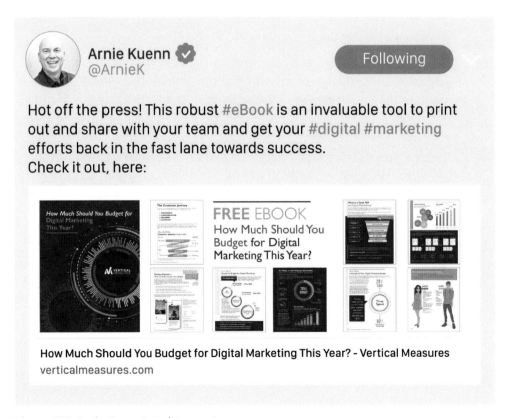

Figure #61: Arnie Kuenn's Twitter post

This post is exactly what you're looking for, but before you can get the free guide, you must provide the following information:

- First and last name
- Email
- Company name
- Job title

You would benefit by gaining access to this content, while Vertical Measures would benefit by getting to know you a little better and getting the chance to offer you related content in the future (which actually benefits us both!). Think about your own company and the advantages you could gain by gating high-quality content:

Benefits of gating content

1. Understand your audience better

By gathering more details about who specifically accessed the content, you can accurately target and nurture those leads in the future.

2. Forge a trusting relationship

Those who invest in gated content by providing their own information likely view the information as valuable, which establishes your brand as trustworthy and authoritative.

3. Streamline your sales process

Conducting outreach to people who accessed your gated content will likely be more effective because you'll have more qualifying information about them.

Drawbacks of gating content

It wouldn't be a fair debate unless both sides are heard. Let's talk about the potential drawbacks of gating content:

1. You might reach a limited audience

It can be harder to get gated content in front of a broad audience unless you put serious effort and budget behind promotion. Depending on your industry and audience needs, it can be difficult to get a large part of your audience to fill out a gated form.

2. It can be harder to earn links

Other websites will typically avoid linking to a gated landing page. This makes sense. Another website may skip sharing gated content out of respect that their audience may not want to give their information to a brand they don't know directly.

3. Some readers might be turned away

Let's face it, gated content can leave a bad taste in a reader's mouth if they find it at the wrong stage of the customer journey or under false pretenses. In these cases, gated content can result in a negative brand perception or even a loss of trust.

Our answer to the great gate debate

Despite the long-winded debates between marketers, the answer to the great gate debate is pretty simple: Gating the wrong content at the wrong time during your customer's journey can discourage potential clients from continued engagement with your brand. However, gating the right content at the right time can help you nurture budding leads into long-term relationships and potentially boost revenue down the road.

Consider this easy formula from Rand Fishkin:

If audience size, reach, and future marketing benefits are greater than detailed leads as a metric or as a value, then you should [provide] open access [content] . If the reverse is true, if detailed leads are more valuable to you than the audience size, the potential reach, the amplification and link, then you should go with a gated model.

Figure #62: Rand Fishkin on gated content

Main Takeaways
& Action Steps

1

List some topic ideas that would provide high value for your customers. Do you have any of this content already?

2

What kinds of supporting topics could help drive incremental traffic to your high-value hub content?

3

What new channels or content formats could you explore to help promote your hub and spoke content?

CHAPTER VII
Sophia reaches a hub landing page and takes an interactive quiz

Creating effective landing pages is essential for any gated content. A strong landing page can help lower bounce rates and get people to provide personal information you can use to nurture them into customers.

Consider Coronado University's landing page for the interactive quiz Sophia discovered earlier:

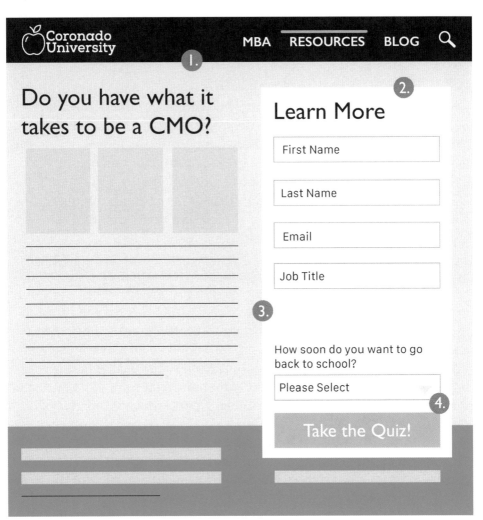

Figure #63: Coronado University Landing Page Example

1. | **Title is optimized to respond to a "need" in the audience.**
The question entices a reader to provide basic information in order to access the content.

2. | **Expectations are clear.**
The landing page doesn't use any bait-and-switch techniques. The reader has a full understanding of what they can expect in exchange for their information.

3. | **Lead capture form is clear and easy to locate.**
The form asks for low-friction information (name, email, job title, and how soon the user wants to go back to school).

4. | **Call to action is bold and clear.**
It doesn't get much clearer than "Take the Quiz!"

What you wouldn't know immediately was that Coronado University was able to rank for the phrase "Do I have what it takes to be a CMO" because that keyword and related phrases are used throughout the copy on the landing page. This means that not only is Coronado tapping into its existing traffic using the Hub & Spoke model, it also is adding an SEO element to each landing page. That helps it rank for the same terms used in the gated content, even though the content itself probably won't be crawled or indexed by search engines since its hidden.

Sophia lands on the quiz landing page from the article she found, and reads the intro copy. The page sets clear expectations about what the quiz will cover, how long it will take to complete and how she can view the results. On top of that, there is related content at the bottom of the page that sparks even more interest for Sophia. Like most of us, Sophia opens several of those related content pieces in separate tabs to read later. She's excited to read an article that discusses the most in-demand industry verticals for chief marketing officers — but that will have to wait until she finishes the quiz.

This is another user behavior consideration. Even though the related topics intrigue Sophia, she's more eager to see if she has the chops to be a CMO first. Even if she left the quiz and explored the content out of order, Sophia would stay engaged with Coronado University's content. The school is helping her along the customer journey.

Now, back to the quiz:

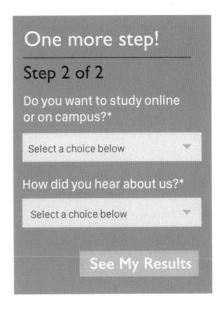

Figure #64: Coronado University Quiz

The quiz is strategically crafted not only to help Sophia learn more about how her goals align with the role of CMO, but also to give Coronado University some very useful information about Sophia.

A few multiple-choice questions include:

- Do you have ambition to lead a team of fellow experienced industry experts?
- What is the lowest compensation you'd be willing to make as CMO?
- What's your current level of education?
- When do you see yourself in an executive marketing role?
- What are your main obstacles at work right now?
- Do you want to study online or on campus?

Think about how useful her answers could be for Coronado University. Not only will the brand start to understand her dreams and pain points, it can also learn how serious she is about going back to school and whether she wants to pursue online classes.

Sophia is directed to a thank you page

After taking this quiz, Sophia is curious about her results. She gives little thought to filling out the last few questions she's asked and clicks "See My Results."

Sophia arrives at a thank you page with her results — she has what it takes! She quickly shares the quiz results on LinkedIn via a share button on the page. Then, she returns to read the other tabs she opened before the quiz. The quiz results and thank you page are enough to make Sophia feel valued and position Coronado University as a helpful resource in her mind. On the back-end, Coronado University received valuable information to continue her customer journey and supply Sophia with more relevant content that could lead her to a decision.

This single piece of content provides the university with critical information it can use to further target Sophia during her journey and deliver even more content to lead her down the funnel. Coronado University learned Sophia loves collaborating with like-minded peers, wants to lead a marketing team on her own and wants to achieve her goals fast.

Sophia has become a qualified lead.

Crafting a thank you page

Thank you pages and confirmation pages are often overlooked yet extremely valuable pages for any brand. Visitors to your thank you page are the next closest thing to a paying customer. Since they've already decided to take the next step along your customer's journey and provided their personal information, these are leads you cannot ignore.

Think about it this way: If your website converts at 5 percent (meaning only five of every 100 visitors even make it to a thank you page), then the visitors who do make it there should be taken seriously!

Thank you pages might look different depending on how you decide to deliver the gated content. For example, you might thank the reader for downloading the gated content, confirm that an email with the content they requested will be sent to the email address provided or, as in Sophia's case, your thank you page might encourage a social action that spreads your content even further.

Here are some thank you page best practices to consider:

Say thanks

Let your visitor know that they completed the form correctly and you're happy that they did. If it's appropriate, congratulate them! Coronado University could certainly congratulate Sophia on her results, for example.

Set clear expectations

Tell users what will happen next. Surprises can be fun in life but are generally bad for business. Inform users about how and when you'll follow up, and then make sure this expectation is met or exceeded. These quick, little wins can go a long way at the beginning of relationships.

Align with their journey

If someone requested more information, a typical next step might involve your sales team reaching out to the newly acquired lead. But it doesn't have to be this way! If a prospect is in a hurry, provide them with an easy way to take the next steps themselves. If they're not ready to convert yet, nurture the lead by providing even more awesome content in an email, as Coronado University will do with Sophia.

Set the right tone

As your audience encounters more and more of your content on their customer journey, setting a consistent tone is just as important as the other steps above. Sending the wrong signals at this stage can undo all the trust you built up until this point. For example, you shouldn't use a casual or flippant tone if your business is very serious.

Understanding interactive content

Interactive content is any of type of digital media that creates a two-way "conversation" with the end user. A website visitor may be able to actively participate with your content through:

- Animated infographics
- Assessments
- Calculators
- Contests
- Games

- Interactive curriculum
- Live chats
- Polls
- Quizzes
- Interactive timelines

For example, the BBC created an extremely engaging webpage that tries to put the vastness of our universe in perspective. As you scroll down the page, a rocket takes flight throughout our solar system, highlighting landmark distances as you pass them. If you scroll in the opposite the direction, the rocket changes course, and you can view other details or information you may have missed. By the end of it you might feel a little dizzy — but also exhilarated.

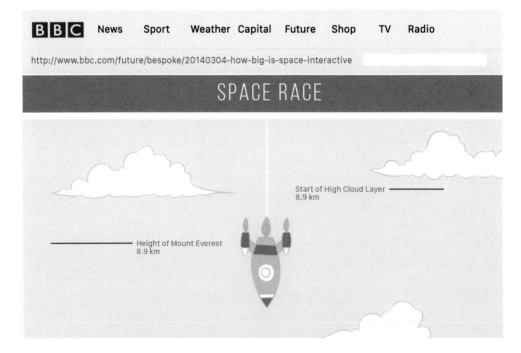

Figure #65: "How Big Is Space? Created by BBC.com

According to data from Playbuzz, 58 percent of marketers say their existing content doesn't create enough opportunity for engagement. That's where the power of interactive content comes in — by definition, it's highly engaging. In contrast, other content types we've listed offer and unresponsive experience, no matter how interesting, insightful, or humorous. Only interactive content allows visitors to turn into users who take action on your website. And it doesn't need to be a trip through space, either. Calculators, infographics, and quizzes like the one Sophia took to learn more about her career options are much more common.

As Scott Brinker, VP of Platform Ecosystem at HubSpot, notes: "By its very nature, interactive content engages participants in an activity: answering questions, making choices, exploring scenarios. It's a great way to capture attention right from the start. Individuals have to think and respond; they can't just snooze through it."

Why use interactive content?

Done well, interactive content can drastically improve conversion rates across your website. In fact, we've had cases where optimizing an existing quiz has improved conversation rates by 130 percent in just one month. In a 2017 study on interactive content from Content Marketing Institute (CMI), the majority of their 20,000 survey respondents agreed that interactive content provides numerous benefits:

 **agree that interactive content grabs attention**

 agree that interactive content enhances retention of brand

 **agree that interactive content can have reusable value, resulting in repeat visitors and multiple exposures**

Forty-six percent of survey respondents to the CMI study said their organization uses some type of interactive content as part of their overall mix of content marketing tactics to engage users. Usage was higher than average among enterprise organizations with more than 1,000 employees, at 63 percent.

What is the purpose of interactive content? According to the CMI survey, marketers use interactive content for:

- Engagement (66%)
- Educating the audience (63%)
- Creating brand awareness (58%)
- Lead generation (57%)
- Conversion (50%)
- Sales/sales enablement (33%)

Interactive content can be highly shareable and, when set up correctly, can even provide opportunities for personalization. With this kind of potential, 88 percent of marketers believe interactive content is an effective way to differentiate a brand, according to Ion Interactive.

These results highlight the growing sophistication of content marketing practices and strategies. Interactive content isn't a direct sales tactic. Rather, it enables organizations to educate their audiences in a way that lets the visitor participate in the experience – a key way to secure engagement and keep people coming back for more.

How to develop interactive content

Upgrade existing content

Everyone cringes at the thought of creating something from scratch. So, try to make it easier! Examine the content you've already created – can you repurpose some of those assets so they become interactive? Could your sales team's product and pricing sheets become online assessments, planners or calculators?

Match interactive content to the customer journey

Determine which types of interactive content will have the greatest impact at specific points in your customer journey:

Collect data

Start by identifying friction points. Where do users tend to abandon your content or your site? Could interactive content keep them engaged?

Run tests

If you're refreshing existing content, pit your old, static version against your new, interactive version. How does behavior and engagement change? Do visitors stay on the page or site longer? Are you earning more authoritative links due to your new, (hopefully) more engaging content?

Manage Costs

Use your tests and results to make wise spending decisions. Avoid investing significant time or resources into too many interactive pieces until you're confident when and how they will drive results. Creating interactive content can be costly, especially if you're starting from scratch.

Find a vendor or software solution

If you don't have internal resources or a freelancer who can help create this kind of dynamic content, consider trying some of the many online tools available:

- apester.com
- brackify.com
- infogram.com
- mapme.com
- riddle.com
- snapapp.com

Main Takeaways
& Action Steps

1

How can you optimize your gate pages to compel users to share personal information in exchange for access?

2

How can you optimize your thank you and confirmation pages to move users further in their customer journey?

3

What kinds of interactive content would your users find valuable?

CHAPTER VIII

Coronado University nurtures Sophia with email

At this point in the journey, Sophia's more than aware of the opportunity to become a CMO — she's interested in learning more and evaluating her options to get started. After handing over some very basic information about herself to access the quiz results, Coronado University is fast at work, creating targeted emails for Sophia that can help lead her further down the sales funnel, closer to enrolling for classes.

You need to own your audience, not rent it!

Most marketers are concerned about getting as many eyeballs on their brand as possible, growing traffic to their website and hoping to see at least a modest return on their marketing investment — if they can track it, that is. Brands often look at marketing as an expense. But what if you could turn your marketing into one of your company's biggest revenue drivers? What if you **owned** the audience instead of **renting** it?

Traditional media is rarely if ever owned. You're essentially renting the print space, billboard or air time on TV or radio to put your content in front of someone else's audience. When you quit paying, the ads disappear, along with much of your brand reach and lead flow. Digital advertising is similar. While it can be easier to track and measure your efforts on digital, you're still paying to rent space on the SERPs, a social platform or someone else's website, hoping to get a click-through to your content. Again, once you quit paying, your content gets evicted from those websites, and your brand is back out on the street.

Organic marketing can come in many forms, including search results, social media mentions, earned links from quality content and so on — but it's not always owned. Why? Didn't you earn those eyeballs? Isn't it free? Well, yes and no. You certainly earned value, as it takes a lot of effort to get organic traffic to your website. But it also isn't free. You spent real time and money to receive that traffic, whether through optimization, loyalty programs or content creation. But when that traffic hits your amazing website, more than 95 percent of it will quickly bounce away, most never to return — still seems **rented**, right?

What is an owned audience?

An audience can be defined as practically anyone who has engaged with your organization, in almost any fashion. An owned audience consists of people who have provided your organization with information you can use to nurture them, such as their name, email address, phone number or job title. Owning your audience might start with something as simple as a visit to your website, but it takes work to get that visitor to buy-in to your brand and become part of your owned audience. For example, Coronado University targeted Sophia with engaging, relevant content that prompted her to provide an email address and other personal information. Sophia is now part of Coronado's owned audience, but not Magellan's.

Here's our view of the audience hierarchy:

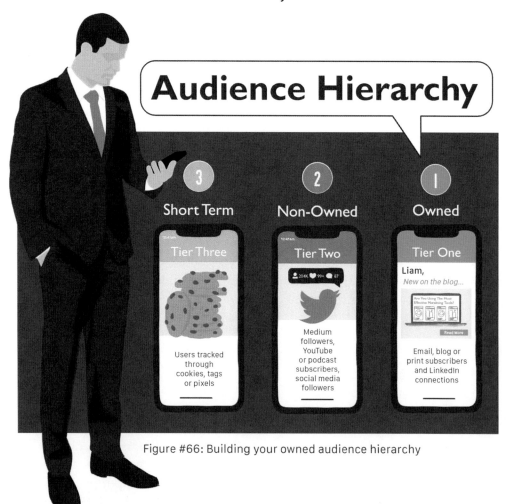

Figure #66: Building your owned audience hierarchy

Why your owned audience is your company's most valuable asset

Remember, the goal is to turn marketing from an expense into a true asset for your company. Building an owned audience can be achieved through many channels – both paid and organic – but once a reader finds your content, it's up to you to capture them.

As mentioned above, most of your marketing money is spent on renting an audience – sometimes for just a second or two – whether that's through traditional media, content optimization, search advertising, social media marketing, guest blogs or industry events. But if you can convert that investment into an owned audience, you're well on your way to building a significant asset for your organization. In fact, according to a Salesforce and LinkedIn study, "The average B2B company has a database of 50,000 individuals and spends an average of $150 to acquire a single email address."[48] That means the email database (their owned audience) alone is worth $7.5 million, which likely makes it the largest asset under a marketer's control, and possibly the company's largest asset overall.

Let's do some math

Figure #67: Putting a value on your owned audience

48 https://a.sfdcstatic.com/content/dam/www/ocms-backup/assets/pdf/datasheets/mc-b2b-perso-nas-targeting-audiences.pdf

Want to build even more value for this asset? There are two main ways to accomplish this:

1. Drive revenue from your owned audience.
2. Drive revenue from renting your own owned audience.

Driving revenue from your owned audience usually requires a quality lead nurture strategy. In fact, an Econsultancy study found that 66 percent of marketers rated email marketing ROI as "excellent or good." Generally, you should nurture top-of-funnel leads along their journey by curating engaging emails with relevant blog posts, videos, eBooks, webinars and other insights that align with their current stage. A harder hitting strategy to drive revenue through email is to offer unique promotions or special offers to your email list or provide early access to new services or products.

Renting your owned audience can also be profitable. The more specialized or unique your audience is, the more potential value you can get for renting access. For example, do you have one of the largest databases of people interested in heavy equipment? You can charge a premium for a heavy equipment rental company to access that audience. To be fair, this might require a different sales effort than you are currently set up for, but the rewards may make it worth adding a sponsorship sales position or something similar.

Putting a value on your owned audience

Trying to determine the value of your owned audience can get complicated, but we'll try to keep it as simple as possible. As mentioned earlier, you could determine the value of your owned audience by how much it cost to earn it. But you can also valuate your owned audience by how much revenue you earn from it.

To determine the value of your owned audience, calculate:

*   What you earn by selling your products or services to your owned audience.
*   What you earn by charging others for access to your owned audience.

The first valuation method requires the right lead nurture tools and some pretty accurate analysis. Basically, you need to measure the value of the products or services the average email subscriber buys from you over a set period of time. Many will use the Lifetime Value (LTV) of an email subscriber as a benchmark. If you know your average subscriber LTV, and you know you have X number of active subscribers, you can multiply the two for your total list value. Another way is to measure how much revenue each of your outreach emails generates each time you send one. A simple example would be sending out emails with an offer that includes a custom tracking code. At the end of the campaign, you can divide the amount of revenue it drove by the number of subscribers who received the email to determine average revenue per subscriber for that outreach effort.

The second valuation method is based on how much revenue you can generate via sponsorships, ads or affiliate fees paid to reach your audience. If you have a list of 40,000 people and charge four sponsors two thousand dollars each for ads in your monthly newsletter, each subscriber is worth $2.40 per year (4 x $2,000 x 12 months = $96,000, divided by 40,000 subscribers). You may even be able to multiply subscriber value, assuming you market to them for a sustained amount of time. Combine your calculations from both methods to estimate a reasonable total value of your owned audience.

Applying effective email marketing to assist your customer's journey

For Coronado University, all their blog articles, promotion efforts and gated content are designed with the end-goal of securing that holy grail — the email address, a new contact added to their owned audience. They now have the power to nurture Sophia toward enrolling as a student in one of their programs, but their work is just starting. It's now their job to consistently meet their owned audience wherever they are in the customer journey and nurture them toward a decision. Today, getting a contact to the decision stage involves a lot of customization and personalization. Email is neither the first nor the last touchpoint between customers and brands. From awareness to decision, email enables your brand to build reputation as a trusted industry leader and showcase the benefits of your product or service. Email helps establish and nurture relationships, build trust and, ultimately, encourage visits to your website that lead to a conversion.

Segmenting your email list

Email segmentation is a crucial first step to meet the needs of your audience. Segmenting your email list lets you adjust your email campaign strategy based on the preferences of specified groups, optimizing the ROI of your efforts. There are many ways you can segment your email list to provide relevant content your audience will enjoy. The more information you collect from your audience at sign-up and over time, the more opportunities you have to message them with emails that resonate.

Coronado University doesn't have a lot of information on Sophia yet. But they do have enough to provide high-quality content that's directly relevant to her. As we all know, personal relevance is central to today's digital consumers, and customers like Sophia demand personalization in order to progress in their journey. For this reason, relevancy is perhaps the most important factor for a successful email marketing campaign.

"Segmented email campaigns get 14.31% more opens and 100.95% more clicks than non-segmented campaigns."

- MailChimp

Geographic segmentation

The first step toward segmenting your audience begins with geography. Segmenting this way is best when your audience's location plays a substantial part in their purchasing decision. For example, Sophia's geographic location might be critical to her decision to go back to school, because she doesn't have the option to relocate her family or travel long distances to continue her education. But, let's assume that you're not in the education vertical. Who else might geographic segmentation work well for?

- Companies that host, sponsor or contribute to local events
- Businesses who operate within certain geographic limitations
- Companies whose products or services only apply to certain geographical areas or climates
- Organizations with a strong connection to or history with a specific location

Behavior-based segmentation

You can also use your audience's behavior as a way to target email messaging and tap into their specific interests or needs. This type of segmentation relies on having the right analytics in place to understand and predict behavior. For example, you will be better able to target an individual who has spent a lot of time on your website and viewed a lot of related content rather than one who bounced quickly off a single service page. If you're using analytics properly, you can differentiate the browsing behavior of different visitors and leverage that information to optimize your emails. In Sophia's case, Coronado University will be able to see the pages she visits, content she downloads and quizzes she completes — actions that help Coronado University create a customer profile it can use to nurture her further down the customer journey.

Content- or interest-based segmentation

Behavior-based segmentation often leads to a clearer understanding of what content your audience is likely to engage with more than others. To segment based on interest, evaluate which content was viewed or downloaded most by your audience. Start by generating a list of people who have downloaded a certain eBook or another piece of gated content, and then segment them into more targeted email or lead nurture campaigns around that topic. These lists can also help identify which content format each audience segment prefers, based on analyzing who consumes more videos, blog posts, webinars, eBooks and other content types.

A visitor might give you their information to access a piece of gated content, but that doesn't mean they actually liked it. Take segmenting and relevancy a step further by building additional lists based on how engaged the members of your owned audience are in specific pieces of content. For example, Coronado University might host an in-depth webinar that covers social media best practices for big brands. In order to access the webinar, users have to sign up on a lead-capture form. After providing their name and email address, these registrants can then be tracked and segmented based on how they engaged with the webinar. If some attendees stayed engaged for the majority of the presentation, Coronado University might re-target them with mid-funnel, consideration-stage content to help move them along in the sales cycle.

Alternatively, if a few attendees dropped off the webinar within the first 10 minutes, they might receive a follow-up email featuring a top-of-funnel offer, or even a feedback survey to gauge what specifically lost their interest.

By using analytics tools, you can track who in your owned audience is spending more or less time with specific types of content. Depending on your findings, you can gauge the interest each individual has in your product, service or industry. Use this information to reinvigorate dwindling interest or push promising leads further down the sales funnel while they're at their most engaged.

We'll show you how Coronado University used this information to re-target Sophia later in this chapter.

Knowledge-level segmentation

Knowledge-level segmentation is based on how much each contact knows about the topics on your blog or website. From there, you can tailor your messaging to deliver content that speaks at the right knowledge level and continue to nurture leads with personalized emails.

Depending on the information you receive from your lead-capture forms and other analytics efforts, you may be able to find out how many degrees your contacts hold or their level of expertise in your specific industry. If you find readers engaging with advanced, technical content, odds are their knowledge on the subject is greater than readers who engage with more basic, entry-level content.

From her answers to the quiz she took, Coronado University knows Sophia's current job title, her desired job title (CMO) and how quickly she wants to achieve it. They know her current education level and that she's leaning toward going back to school online. The way Coronado University will target her moving forward depends heavily on this information. Its messaging to Sophia will differ significantly from the way it messages prospects with more or less years of experience, an interest in nursing or a desire to attend college on campus full-time. At the same time, they'll nurture Sophia with additional content that can help them learn more about her, such as her salary and budget for continuing education, her living situation or her biggest fears about going back to school.

Industry- or role-based segmentation

Whether you're in the B2B or B2C space, you might encounter contacts in your email list from many different industries and job roles. Speaking to these differences can add another level of personalization to your email marketing campaigns.

Segmenting your audience by position or industry can have a big impact on how readers interpret and engage with your content. For example, Coronado University will engage differently with Sophia than another contact based solely her job title and industry. She's a mid-level marketer. She's currently working for a marketing agency and holds a related college degree. They know she's not interested in nursing degrees or healthcare-related content and that her experience and level of interest demands content that's high-level and relatively advanced.

Brand-advocacy segmentation

If you take away anything from our overview on email segmentation, it's this: Brand and customer loyalty must be cultivated. Always.

Sofia isn't close to being a brand advocate for Coronado University — yet — but one of their segmented lists includes many brand advocates, including:

- Alumni
- Social media fans
- Current students who have recommended the school to others
- Non-students who have advocated for the school's programs online

After building a list of advocates related to your business, such as frequent buyers, vocal fans or business partners, start tailoring emails to acknowledge and thank them. Reach out to them for feedback and notify them first about new services or products, special rewards, or perks to show how much you appreciate their support.

Hello,

Kristen from Wistia here! I'm writing you today to give you a sneak peak at some exciting changes coming to Soapbox.

We'll soon announce that we're converting **Soapbox Pro** to two different plans: **Soapbox Solo & Soapbox for Teams.** You're among the early adopters who bought Soapbox Pro accounts for multiple people, so we're transitioning you over to the teams plan at your current price/seat, for as long as you're with us.

Consider yourself grandfathered. 😊

No action is required on your part, and you'll be getting some new sweet features. For all the deets, watch my 3.5 min video:

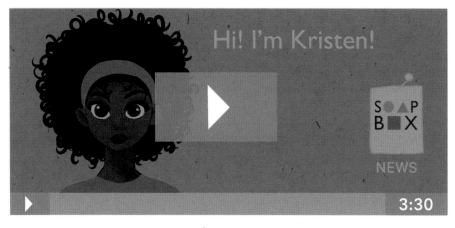

Soapbox Pro ▶ Soapbox for Teams

We're pumped about our vision of making Soapbox a more collaborative tool for teams and hope you are too. As always, feel free to reply to this email with your thoughts on features that would enhance your Soapbox experience!

Figure #68: Example email targeted for advocates (Source: Soapbox)

By segmenting your brand advocates, you can not only try to increase their overall LTV, but also reward their loyalty to increase their advocacy of your brand. Remember, with list segmentation, the goal isn't to generate leads — you've already got those. The goal is to nurture your leads into long-term customers.

How to create and optimize successful email campaigns

Let's jump ahead. You've segmented your audience into a few lists, planned out several email workflows, and started building your emails. How do you know they will resonate with your targeted audiences? How do you compel them to open your emails in the first place, when there may be dozens or even hundreds of unopened messages in their inboxes already?

"On any given day, the average customer will be exposed to 2,904 media messages, will pay attention to 52 and will positively remember only four."

- SuperProfile

One of the best ways to ensure your emails are opened by a targeted audience is to show them that you understand their needs and priorities. Sounds pretty familiar to content marketing, right? Show your audience that you know who they are, what they care about and how they think. Most of the time, people's response to this notion is, "That sounds creepy." But they are dead wrong.

There's a balance between being creepy and being personable and well-informed. There's a way to message your audience in a way that says, "I understand what your problems are, and believe I can help you solve them." This type of messaging goes beyond personalizing an email with someone's name. Utilize the demographic and behavioral data we've covered previously to create attention-grabbing emails that cut right to the chase. As much as we'd like to send the same message to everyone (how easy that would be!), mass marketing simply isn't effective anymore. You need to find more ways to customize your messages to targeted audiences. Here's how:

Create a killer subject line

Emails need to grab the reader's attention, and that starts with a killer subject. The subject is one of only a few pieces of information your audience will take into consideration when deciding whether or not to open your email in the first place, along with the sender and preview text. According to Convince & Convert, 35 percent of email recipients open their email based on the subject line alone.[49]

Subject lines should be concise and informative, setting a clear expectation on why a user should click through. This might seem obvious, but unfortunately, it can be difficult. Spend time crafting these all-important one liners. But beware! Clickbait-y titles could cost you in the long run, even if they get some people to open your email initially. Keeping your subject lines straightforward and to the point helps people learn what to expect from you so they stay engaged, rather than immediately clicking unsubscribe because of a manipulative bait-and-switch subject.

Your subject lines should first and foremost address your reader's concerns. If Coronado University wants to send an email to a list of mid-level marketers like Sophia, and they know that one of her primary challenges is not having enough time in her day to complete projects, the school might use a subject line that says, "Want to save time in your marketing processes?" This subject line addresses Sophia's pain point while adding a value proposition (save time), creating the impression that Coronado University can help her solve her problem. In addition to questions, you can use CTAs in your subject lines to inspire action, such as "join," "get," "explore," "download," and other active verbs.

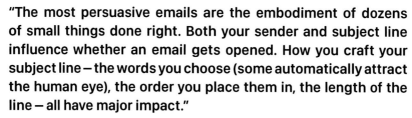

"The most persuasive emails are the embodiment of dozens of small things done right. Both your sender and subject line influence whether an email gets opened. How you craft your subject line — the words you choose (some automatically attract the human eye), the order you place them in, the length of the line — all have major impact."

- Nancy Harhut, Chief Creative Officer HBT Marketing

49 https://www.convinceandconvert.com/convince-convert/15-email-statistics-that-are-shaping-the-future/

Cut the fat

It's not just your subject lines that need to be clear and concise. The meat of your emails should be lean, too. It's a delicate balance for most marketers. How can you make an email informative and engaging, but also reduce reading time? The trick is cutting the fat from your copy and focusing on messages that get right to the point, whether its new information you need to share or an action you want the reader to take.

MarketingProfs
Smart thinking...pass it on.

Hi Colleague,

I just wanted to give you a heads up that the PRO Member Early Bird Rate for the B2B Forum 2019 expires Saturday, April 30.

If you register before May 1, you'll save $400 on your Forum registration. Just think of what that extra money could go toward instead – half of an iPad 2, a new business causal outfit for Boston, or a round of top-shelf drinks at the hotel bar (oh wait, I guess I'd be the one to benefit from that). **REGISTER NOW**

See you in Boston,

Ann

Ann Handley
Chief Content Officer
MarketingProfs
Tweet This Conference!

Figure #69: Example of concise, compelling email copy (Source: MarketingProfs)

We love this example from MarketingProfs because the language is direct and conversational – it actually reads like a human wrote it. It uses short paragraphs and formatting to break up the text visually, so it's easy to scan and digest. We've all become seasoned skim-readers. No one wants to read an essay in their inbox these days, so if your email looks like a college thesis (no offense, Coronado University), readers will lose interest before they even start reading. Cut the fat!

"4 out of 10 email subscribers reported that they've marked emails as spam simply because they were irrelevant."

-MarketingSherpa

Strong images are worth a thousand emails

Like any other piece of content, your emails should be visually compelling. Strong imagery plays a very important role in attracting a viewer's attention when they open your emails and enticing them to click through to a relevant piece of content that can lead them through the customer journey.

Stock imagery sucks. We all know it. As easy as it might be to pick out a random stock photograph of two men shaking hands, it's an awful choice for your emails. A much more effective strategy is to have imagery that is just as relevant as the body copy.

Figure #70: Example email with strong imagery (Source: Warby Parker)

Create clear calls-to-action

As with any piece of content you create, emails should include a clear CTA for users. The CTA is arguably one of the most important aspects of an email's performance because it can directly impact click-through. Let's get real: The entire reason you're spending all this time creating personas, segmenting audiences, drafting compelling copy and making awesome imagery is, ultimately, to get people to do something – right? Eventually, you want to get them to a landing page where they can convert into a paying customer. That takes a great CTA.

ADVENTURE CO.

The Desert is Calling and You Must Go...

The desert is calling... Experience the desert like never before. Earn and redeem adventure points for your next expedition! Share time with fellow wanderers while trekking the greatest trails in the southwest.

Book My Adventure

Figure #71: Sample email with clear call-to-action

How do you create a compelling enough CTA that people will click the link and convert? To start, always select one CTA for your emails – not two, not three. One. Limit the number of places a reader can go from your email. If you offer too many choices or links, readers could easily get confused about what to do next or skip taking any action at all. Narrow the purpose of the email to one primary action you want your readers to take.

The design of your CTA matters, too. Whether it's a graphic button or an embedded link, you want to make sure the CTA is prominent and visually distinct from the rest of the copy. Of course, the whole email design should align with the rest of your branding, down to the voice and tone.

Your CTA should be the clear focus of your email, so make it stand out and draw the reader's eye. Try to keep CTAs "above the fold" of the message so readers can see them quickly without having to scroll down. Odds are, very few recipients will scroll through your email, especially if the benefit to them isn't clearly highlighted in the subject line. You should use copy that is clear and action-oriented throughout your emails, but especially in CTAs.

For example:

Action-oriented:
Download your copy, Read our reviews, Take a stand

Urgent:
Get the scoop, Claim your limited offer, Shop the sale

Friendly:
Join us, Share your story, Learn more

"Triggering the Scarcity Principle, the Availability Bias, Social Proof or any of a number of other behavioral science principles can make a huge difference in how persuasive your message is. Will someone feel they'll miss out if they don't open the email? Will they feel the sender's described a situation they can readily call to mind? Will they get the sense that people like them are interested in the message?"

- Nancy Harhut

Another way to optimize your CTAs is to include multiple links or buttons throughout your email that all point to the same landing page. This approach offers your readers more opportunities to click-through when and how they want to.

The human connection

Like every stage in the customer journey, your overarching goal for email campaigns is to build a trusting relationship with your readers that eventually leads to a conversion. Human connection is powerful, and it's evident when we look at email performance. Email marketing should be a personalized experience — send your emails from an actual person from your staff!

You might also consider including a small picture of the sender with their signature if they're comfortable with the idea. Even a simple headshot of the person sending the email helps support a more personable approach to email. Set a friendly, approachable tone that reinforces the idea of starting a conversation with a real human, not an emotionless marketing production line.

What if you have multiple senders for your email campaigns? Test them! See which sender generates the most engagement with your emails. You might assume that sending emails from the CEO of your company is most effective, but what if you're promoting a specific piece of content and it makes more sense to send an email from the author? Like everything else in digital marketing, email campaigns should be tested and measured so you can continually iterate and improve.

Make emails easily shareable

There's no shame in hoping your audience might help promote emails for you. In fact, that should be one of your goals! Always encourage your readers to share your content. At this point in your digital marketing journey, that should be a no-brainer. Luckily, a lot of the same basic rules apply for email marketing. By making it easier for email recipients to share your offers, newsletters, announcements and information with their networks, you can expand your reach and broaden the opportunity to generate new leads.

Since you're sending emails to segments of your existing contact list, you're not going to generate any new leads from email unless you make it easy to share the content. If your contacts share your content with people who aren't in your database and they end up converting, you've landed some new leads with minimal effort. All you have to do is include social sharing links in all your emails.

Hopefully by now you have a clear understanding of which social networks your audience segments frequent most. Include links for Facebook, Twitter, LinkedIn, Pinterest or whichever network applies to your audience at the top and bottom of your emails. You can also include an email-forward link, which is another great way to encourage your readers to share your content and help you generate new leads.

Mobile optimization is critical

You might be able to relate to this: Have you ever opened an email on your phone and the formatting was so messed up you could barely read it? The text was either too large or too small, and the images never fit your screen — pretty annoying, right? I'm willing to bet you quickly deleted the email and may not even remember the brand that sent it. Don't make your readers deal with that same issue when they look at your emails! Optimize your emails so they display nicely across all devices.

Properly designed and optimized emails should adapt to whatever device your readers use. To make it easier, build your emails using responsive templates to ensure your readers have the best experience digesting your email content and taking action.

"About 3 in 5 consumers check their email on the go (mobile) and 75% of say they use their smartphones most often to check email."

– Fluent

Don't get overwhelmed. Today's email service providers make it easy to create email content that displays properly across devices. And if you follow the rest of the advice in this chapter, you'll start seeing an increase in your click-through and conversion rates before you know it.

The right to unsubscribe

Plain and simple: It's illegal not to include an unsubscribe link in your email sends. But that's not the only reason why you shouldn't send emails without an unsubscribe option. Think about it this way: Why would you want to send emails to uninterested recipients? Let's pretend that Tennessee Mountain Winery sends out a monthly newsletter to subscribers for their latest deals, wine of the month club, tour openings and other events. You were subscribed a few years ago when you visited Nashville and toured their vineyard for your anniversary. You keep getting emails from Tennessee Mountain Winery without the option to unsubscribe. For months, you've sent each and every email directly to your spam or trash folder because you don't live in Nashville and, quite frankly, you have no intention of ordering cases of their wine. All you wanted from them was single trip to their vineyard. You accomplished that — four years ago — and now it's unlikely that you'd ever go back, even if you lived in Nashville!

How does it benefit Tennessee Mountain Winery to keep sending emails? At this point, they should see that you haven't opened or converted from one of their emails in four years. And while it's a small sample size, they're actually hurting their email campaign's performance by sending emails to you. The metrics they should be tracking will be directly affected, because they refuse (or scared) to take me off the email list.

If someone's not interested in getting your emails, don't force them to be on your list. Give them an unsubscribe option. Keep your open and click-through rates more accurate and give yourself a better chance to convert engaged segments of your audience. We're not suggesting that you make the unsubscribe option as prominent as your call-to-action, but don't hide it, either. This has everything to do with user experience. Trust us, members of your audience will remember if you keep them hostage in your email list. If they're looking to unsubscribe from your emails and can't find that button, they will most likely mark you as spam, which puts your sender reputation at risk and could seriously impact your email campaign performance.

The unsubscribe option doesn't have to be treated like a defeat, either. One of our favorite unsubscribe tactics is to do it with some personality. You can always try to keep people on your list by providing a fun, enticing or unique option to re-subscribe. This approach can help reduce the likelihood that they'll leave your list, but every reader has a right to choose for themselves.

• We miss you already... •

Hi Friend,

We love that you're subscribed to HubSpot's Marketing Blog, but we noticed you haven't clicked on an email from us in a long time. We totally get it: Our eyes (and subscription habits) are often bigger than our capacity to read everything.

We don't want to add clutter to your inbox, so we're going to stop sending you emails from HubSpot's Marketing Blog.

But we are a little worried about how you'll keep up with the latest marketing trends, tips, and best practices, since you'll you missing out on awesome articles like:

- 25 of the Best PowerPoint Presentation Examples Every Marketer Should See
- How to Teach Yourself SEO in 30 Days
- 15 of the Best job Interview Questions to Ask Candidates

Our subscribers also get exclusive access to new templates, research, and tools before anyone else. If that sounds appealing, click here to re-subscribe.

RE-SUBSCRIBE NOW

See you soon?

Karla Cook,
Editor, HubSpot Marketing Blog

Figure #72: Fun re-subscribe email example

Don't be afraid to
cut ties with unengaged contacts

As important as the unsubscribe button is to your users, it's also a valuable tool for you as a marketer. It's sort of like getting dumped in high school – it seems like the hardest thing ever, but letting go is the best option in the long run. To preserve your reputation, you need to move on from subscribers who can't be bothered to click on your CTAs or even open the emails in the first place.

Before letting these contacts go, try to get some closure. Send at least one or two emails with special incentives, offers or information that can act as a reactivation campaign to give them one last chance. After all, cultivating existing customers is five times cheaper than trying to acquire new ones, according to Experian.[50] If there's still no sign of engagement after this re-engagement, it's time for you to move on and find someone who is more attentive to your emails.

Determining email frequency

Every marketer tries to avoid the spam folder. It's the pit of doom for creative messaging that you worked so hard to create. Every marketer wants recipients to open their emails and read the content. You spent time crafting that perfect subject line, writing compelling copy and adding relevant imagery, but your content is getting caught by these annoying (albeit vital) spam filters. Why?

According to a recent survey by MarketingSherpa, 91 percent of American respondents actually said they want promotional emails.[51] If someone signed up for your list, they're interested in your business, products and services or the information you have to offer. So, if you're not doing anything shady but still getting flagged as spam, the problem might have less to do with the type of emails you're sending and more with how often you send. Before you can figure out that all-important sweet spot for email frequency, you must take a careful look at what you've been doing so far in the email campaign. If you're using an email marketing platform, such as MailChimp, Emma, HubSpot or anything else, you should have some analytics tools at your disposal.

---

50 https://www.uk.experian.com/assets/marketing-services/white-papers/
wp-reactivation-programme.pdf

51 https://www.marketingsherpa.com/article/chart/how-customers-want-promo-emails

To measure past email success and determine the proper email frequency, consider tracking the following metrics:

- Open rate
- Click-through rate
- Unsubscribe rate

Almost everything you need to know is hidden in these numbers. Look at your most highly engaged subscribers to find out how often they're opening emails and when. Use this information to decide how many emails you send each month, and which days your emails perform best. Generally, we've found the best day to send an email is Tuesday, but that may not be true for your specific industry or audience. While sending emails on Tuesdays might give you a good starting place to establish a baseline, as we've discussed earlier in this chapter, effective email is all about targeting your specific audience segments. Depending on each segment, you might see better performance on different days of the week and with different frequency of email. At the very least, however, you should send one email a month, or your subscribers will forget about you. According to the same MarketingSherpa survey, 86 percent of people would like to receive promo emails at least monthly. If you wait longer than that, this survey suggests, you'll be rebooting your relationship with them from scratch every time you send a new email.

So, how can you track the success of your past emails to know how you can improve for the future?

Measuring the success of your emails

Email marketing platforms offer robust measurement capabilities that make it easy to track various metrics that clearly illustrate email performance. With these metrics, you can establish goals specific to your needs, discover the best cadence for emails, learn which type of content performs best and more. Here are the most critical metrics to keep an eye on for your next email marketing campaign:

Total opens

Total opens shows the number of recipients who open each email. It's important to closely monitor this metrics to better understand the content that resonates most with recipients. Take it a step further and compare the total number of opens between mobile and desktop devices to see where and how your audience is engaging with you.

"55% of those emails are opened on a mobile device, and only 16% are opened on a desktop computer."

- Return Path

Open rates

Open Rate is the total number of times an email is opened divided by the total number of emails sent. This results in a clear percentage of emails opened for each email campaign. An increase in open rates can be a sign that your content is resonating well with your audience, and you might notice that click-through rates, conversions and overall revenue from your email rise, as well. Pay close attention to what subject lines, imagery and copy were used for emails with the highest open rates. This information will give a clear blueprint on the type of content your audience wants in their emails.

"From a sample of more than 25 million emails, the average open rate across all industries is 37%."

- HubSpot

Total click-through rate (CTR)

Your CTR is the number of times a click is made within an email divided by the total impressions. Impressions, in this case, is the total number of people who received the email in their inbox. The CTR is so important for marketers because it can tell you a lot about your content's performance. It helps determine if your CTA is compelling enough to inspire action. If your open rate is high but the CTR of your emails is low, then it's likely that your email list is engaged with your company but wasn't interested in your recent email's content.

> **"The median click-through rate in the world is 2.3%, in the U.S. 2.2%. The education, healthcare, retail and consumer products/services verticals performed the best out of all 14 industries analyzed in the post when it came to their click-through rates. The consumer products industry had the highest median click thru rate of 3.3%."**
>
> - MarketingProfs

Abuse reports

Abuse reports indicate the rate your email list subscribers marked a specific email as spam. Of all the metrics for email, this is the one you should never be excited to see. Although there could be many reasons a person might consider your email spammy, these reports are a clear indication that the messaging or strategy behind your emails needs a long, hard look. If your emails continue being reported as spam, you'll notice a steady increase in unsubscribe rates and disengaged contacts.

It's impossible to maintain a list of contacts with 100 percent engagement, but it is possible to avoid abuse reports from most of your audience. To help with this, always offer a one-click unsubscribe option and continue searching for that sweet-spot of email frequency to avoid overwhelming your audience with too many emails.

Bounce Rate

Bounce rate for email is a bit different than bounce rate for web pages. An email bounce rate is defined as an email that doesn't pass the recipient's mail server and therefore never lands in their inbox. Monitor your emails regularly and note whether any content in your emails is triggering email servers to block them or send them to spam folders. Factors might include too many links, confusing subject lines, different symbols or languages in the body copy, etc.

It's important to understand the difference between a hard- and soft-bounce. If a user switches to another email service provider or changed jobs from where their email address originated, this would be considered a hard-bounce. Alternatively, a soft-bounce is typically due to a temporary situation, like the email server is down or the recipient's email inbox is full. HubSpot's Manager of Content Marketing Strategy, Ginny Soskey, recommends that you keep your total bounce rate under 2 percent. This can be accomplished by removing hard-bounce addresses as soon as you can, keeping an eye for those in the soft-bounce list and optimizing email content to avoid general spam filters.

> **"The average bounce rate for college and university websites was 51% in 2018."**
>
> – OHO Interactive

Unsubscribe Rate

Unsubscribe rate counts subscribers who removed themselves from your email list. This metric is a strong indicator of how your messaging is perceived by your audience. While there are many ways to minimize your email unsubscribe rate, it typically boils down to the best practices we covered earlier in this book. What messaging does your audience want from your business? What type of content are they looking for? Are you offering valuable resources in your email to keep them engaged and wanting more? Staying aligned with these interests should keep your unsubscribe rate at manageable levels. If your list receives less than a 2 percent unsubscribe rate, we consider that typical for most verticals. If the unsubscribe rate is higher, however, it might be time to rethink your approach.

78% of consumers have unsubscribed from emails because a brand was sending too many emails.

– HubSpot

Email Conversions

An email conversion is when a specific email leads a subscriber to take a desired action. This could include downloading a piece of content, registering for a webinar, or even making a purchase. Tracking these conversion rates helps decipher how much you of your budget should be spent on email marketing. Because after all, if your audience isn't converting through email, it's in your best interest to adjust the marketing budget to deliver the best ROI.

"Nurtured leads have a 23% shorter sales cycle."

– Market2Lead

Email Revenue

Similarly, email revenue is measured by the total revenue generated from your individual emails.

A lack of email revenue would be a clear indication to stop spending more time and resources on email marketing for your business. But, what if you're generating some revenue from your email but want to improve? As the common mantra goes, it's easier to keep a customer than to obtain a new one. Cater to your existing customers with targeted email campaigns — these are the people who are most likely to convert.

Target your existing customers to keep them engaged with your messaging and interested in your product or services. Using the information you already have on your audience, consider sending surveys, promotions or birthday emails. If one of your products needs to be replenished, such as beauty products, yearly subscriptions or even groceries, send automated follow-ups. Just from these follow-ups alone, you can encourage the recipient to purchase from your website again — adding to email revenue.

"The average ROI of lead nurture is $44 for every $1 spent."

- Campaign Monitor 2016 Annual Report

How privacy regulations impact email marketing

Ever been chatting with your friends on Facebook and an ad in the margin catches your eye for the exact pair of hiking boots you had shopped for on Amazon last week? Or how about that time you were flipping through your email inbox and in pops a Pinterest update with the perfect idea for your 8-year-old daughter's birthday party — how do they know these things? The answer is simple: because you told them.

Whether you specifically asked for information or visited a webpage and showed interest in a product or service, you were telling that brand everything they needed to know: what you do and don't have interest in. This personal and behavioral information is invaluable, particularly to us marketers, because we're always looking for better ways to target emails. Because audiences are much more likely to engage with a brand that understands where their last engagement left off, this information allows for sequential messaging that's more useful to consumers. This is because the information is based on their recent behavior rather than the "shotgun" method of showing a generic ad to as many users in a market as possible.

We're sure you're saying,

"Great! More relevant email sounds nice and efficient, what's the problem?"

Well, for every example of a brand using user data to better target messaging, there's at least one example of a company abusing that privilege. Like brands selling your personal data to third parties without asking, or companies that don't protect your personal information well enough to prevent external breaches.

"That's horrible! But isn't that old news?"

Sort of. A new set of revised privacy regulations in the European Union significantly affect the ways brands can collect, store and use the personal data that allows for sophisticated retargeting messages. The rules should make it easier for consumers to see what a brand keeps in terms of your personal information, and should force brands to quickly report when their data has been compromised, and implement more extensive penalties for brands not adhering to the regulations. More specifically, the General Data Protection Regulation (GDPR).

One of the questions our clients ask most, whether they're marketing rookies or masters, is how they can avoid the pitfalls of the recent GDPR. After all, building a quality email marketing list takes time, patience, and a verifiable sign-up process. Getting people's permission to send them your marketing campaigns not only complies with anti-spam regulations, but it also ensures you're cultivating an audience that's loyal to your brand.

"So, what in the heck is GDPR?"

GDPR is a landmark EU privacy compliance regulation that started May 25, 2018. The new rules apply to any business marketing goods or services, or more specifically the collection and storage of personal identifiers, to individuals based in the EU.

Here's a list of the new expectations these rules are designed to ensure:

Breach notification:

Any breach must be reported "without undue delay" to all customers that were affected.

Right to access:

A copy of all personal data being housed for any user must be provided for free at the request of the user.

Right to be forgotten:

The right of the user to ask that all their data be purged from a system on request.

Data portability:

The right of the user to ask that their personal data be moved to another data controller.

Privacy by design:

A requirement for all data controllers to hold and process ONLY the data necessary for completing an on-site or off-site action as well as minimizing internal access to user data to only those required to process.

Data protection officers:

An individual tasked with ensuring adherence to the new privacy rules, training any staff involved with handling user data, and conducting data audits. In a larger setting this person may be a new hire but in a smaller setting, this can be an existing staff member who would assume these tasks.

Users will have new rights pertaining to when and where their information has been harvested, how it's being used, and most importantly, if it has been compromised in any way. Anyone remember any of the last few enterprise-level data breaches?

Yahoo (2013-2014):	eBay (2014):	Target (2013):	Uber (2016):	Facebook (2018):
3B	**145M**	**110M**	**57M**	**50M**
3 billion user accounts compromised	145 million user accounts compromised	110 million user accounts compromised	57 million users had personal information exposed	50 million user accounts exposed

And on it goes…

Were any of you affected by one of the above? How did you find out? You found out weeks or months later when the company finally admitted the breach, right? This is a great example of what the GDPR will try to stop. Under the new standards, a user has certain rights to know when and where a breach occurs with enough time to do something proactive about it. While the United States does not currently feature GDPR-style regulations applying to U.S. residents, it will observe the GDPR standards as they relate to EU citizens. If you do business with anyone who lives in the countries of the EU, you must follow these rules now. In addition, it's highly likely the United States and others (United Kingdom, Canada) will develop and approve a similar, if not the same, style of privacy regulations in the very near future. Getting to know and preparing your site and emails for these potential changes is highly recommended.

This isn't intended to stop marketing or to stop advertising, but to make it easier for a user to understand when, where, and how their information is being used or misused. That said, we marketers have a little more work to do in order to make sure this gets done. While some of the regulations and how they may apply to a U.S.-based business are still in a gray area, here are a few things we recommend for your emails and website.

I. Cookie Notice & Cookie Preference Center

Brands must do a better job of informing a user how their personal information might be used and allow each site user access to customize what personal data is and isn't tracked. For example, ever seen a notice like this (see below)?

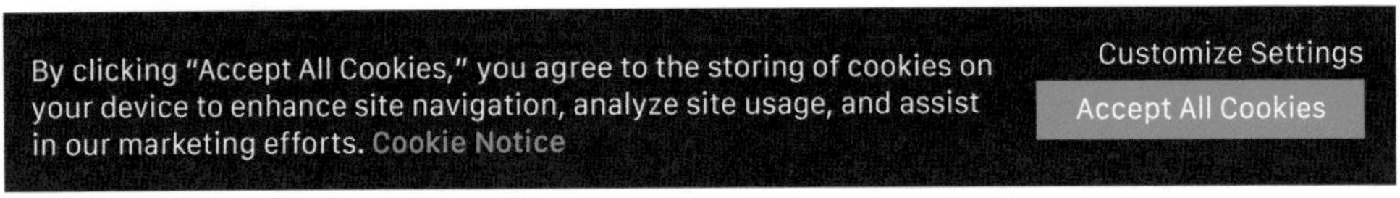

By clicking "Accept All Cookies," you agree to the storing of cookies on your device to enhance site navigation, analyze site usage, and assist in our marketing efforts. Cookie Notice

Customize Settings

Accept All Cookies

Figure #73: Example "Accept All Cookies" notice

This is an essential step and should post for all new users and returning users outside of a typical cookie storage window. This allows new audiences to agree to private data storage for marketing purposes as well as returning audiences to re-submit their approval.

We also strongly recommend installing a Cookie Preference Center option to ensure 100 percent adherence to GDPR standards. A preference center is what gives a user the ability to research which specific user information may be collected and how that information may be used, as well as the ability to selectively accept or refuse individual cookie tactics. A preference center module should also allow you to report on user cookie settings across multiple browsers and provide a historical record of individual user consent over time. The latter could become particularly useful during any scenario where a user submits a complaint.

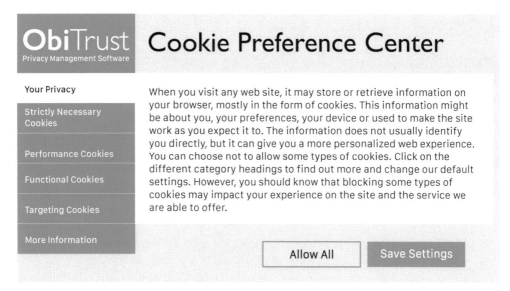

Figure #74: Example "Cookie Preference Center"

The above recommendations for notifying users and giving them the ability to opt-in and -out of specific tracking activities encompasses our full GDPR compliance recommendations to ensure your cookie and retargeting activities remain lawful yet effective.

2. Submission-form "Bill of Rights"

Right below any of your user-facing form fills, you should document what information you are collecting and how it will be used, along with a link to your brands privacy policy. Adding a checkbox increases the likelihood a user will commit to the end result.

Fields marked with an * are required

Name

Email

This form collects your name and email so that we can add you to our newsletter list for awesome project updates. Check out our **privacy policy** for the full story on how to protect and manage your submitted data!

☐ **I consent to having BRAND collect my name and email***

Submit

Figure #75: Submission form adhering to GDPR regulations

Will you lose conversions? Yes, most likely because you are adding points of friction to the sign-up process. An intended consequence, however, is that those who check the box and submit their information may be more expectant of any future correspondence (email, search, social, video) and that will, in turn, increase your overall click-through rate during future engagements. In other words — lower conversion volume in favor of higher engaged conversions — everyone's dream, right?

3. User Data Storage

It will become very important to quickly and easily send a digital file detailing personal data for any user should they request it. This may require new back-end systems, processes or personnel, but whatever the cost, make sure it's a function you have going forward.

While GDPR regulations do not currently apply to U.S. citizens, understanding how it will impact EU audiences, as well as where U.S. regulations may be following, will give you a leg-up on remaining privacy-compliant. Keep in mind, these changes should help improve advertising-audience relations as we, as brands and agencies, only want to provide answers and protect user data in the process. Adhering to these standards could result in lower impression volume overall, but the impressions that remain should be more well informed of what to expect going forward from each brand they interact with, and that means higher engagement!

We recommend adding new email subscribers through a double opt-in process. This process usually includes a sign-up form accompanied with an automated confirmation email. It's a simple extra step that ensures you get the necessary permission from subscribers, and so all recipients have clear expectations on what type of emails you'll be sending, as well as how often.

Sophia clicks on a spoke article from Coronado University's email

Those folks over at Coronado sure have a winning strategy. Not only have they nurtured Sophia this far in her journey, they've now set up an automated lead flow that targets her with relevant content through email. At this point, she's focused on the end goal and often daydreams about the exciting road ahead. Her phone vibrates at work — it's a newsletter from Coronado University, addressed directly to Sophia.

The email (acting as a spoke) is designed to push her further along toward making a decision, but for Sophia, something valuable catches her eyes.

> At this stage, users are looking for tangible information that can help them make a decision.
>
> They evaluate:
>
> - What's the commitment?
> - Am I getting enough value for the price?
> - What exactly am I getting myself into?

Every piece of content you create should have a purpose. And there should be no dead ends. The Coronado University newsletter included news about the school's monthly events, testimonials from fellow students and a really intriguing eBook called, "Career Spotlight: Following the Top CMOs in America." Sophia assesses the cost to get the guide and decides she's willing to exchange more of her personal information for it. After all, Coronado University has produced several pieces of useful content for her — she's beginning to rely on that trusting relationship.

The gate page asks a single, low-friction question: "How serious are you about becoming a Chief Marketing Officer?" This is fairly simple for Sophia to answer — she's pretty serious by now — and that information helps Coronado University immensely. They now know her timeline to possibly enroll. The school is even better positioned to target her as she continues her journey into the decision stage.

Main Takeaways
& Action Steps

1

Do you currently have an owned audience? If so, can you calculate its value? If not, how can you develop one?

2

Are you tracking the efforts of your email campaigns? What are you currently doing with that information?

3

What strategies outlined in this chapter can you use to optimize your lead nurture campaigns?

CHAPTER IX
Eager to learn more, Sophia refines her search again

Sophia reads the eBook, and her journey gains more momentum. From the eBook, she learns what CMOs earn, where they are in most demand, what skills they need and what roles they play in the industry. Some of this was repeat info to her, but she felt that was good to clarify her understanding of things.

Sophia completed extensive research on her education options, and is close to entering the final stage of her journey. She has most of the information, but is still looking for something that will validate her choice of going back to school. At the end of the eBook, the call-to-action is a form to request more information directly from representatives at Coronado University. Shortly after filling out the RFI form with her phone number, Sophia is contacted by the admissions department.

The call from Coronado University's admissions department is the first time she's directly spoken to someone from the school. Think about that for a second. It's been months since she was initially introduced to Coronado's content. It's been months since Magellan University dropped out of contention due to a gap in content. All this research was completed before ever talking to a salesperson or representative from an online university. That's a factor that can easily get lost when strategizing around the customer journey. All your prospects and customers turn to the internet to investigate their next purchase. They're not waiting to get your mailer, see your advertisement, or talk to you at a trade show. They shop when they are ready, not when you are ready. It's getting easier and easier for people to find what they want online. Whether a consumer wants to buy a rotary encoder or a calibration instrument, hire an employee benefits agency or get their online MBA, they want to make an informed decision.

- What are the costs?
- How do different brands compare?
- What features are available, and which are really worth it?
- Is this even the best way to approach my problem?

Consumers have so many questions, yet many companies still do not get this basic content marketing concept. They're not trying to help users make informed decisions; they're just trying to get people to buy their stuff. It's not surprising that so many potential online customers are cynical, suspicious and weary. They have their own concerns, needs and priorities, none of which are your brand. Or your mission statement. Or your value proposition. Or your limited-time offer.

So, why do so many brands focus exclusively on the heavy marketing pitch? Why exhaust word count on their sales copy instead of speaking more to the customer's needs and pain points? For every person actively considering your product or service, there are 10 or 100 or 1000 other folks with a question or need that will lead them there in time.

Questions and reservations are obstacles between your prospects and your brand. Remove those obstacles before the sale. Answer the questions, even the tough ones. Especially the tough ones. If you don't, someone else will, and that competitor will be closer to earning customer trust. When that prospect's questions and reservations have all been answered, you can have all the top rankings in Google you like — you're now competing with the brand who's been holding that prospect's hand the whole way. The brand that truly understands them.

Some of the searches Sophia might make in this stage revolve around finding the answers needed to make her final decision. Sophia feels stronger about getting her MBA with a concentration in marketing after her discussion with Coronado University's admissions department. Equipped with a deeper understanding of advanced marketing career paths and fewer questions, her inner dialogue asks, 'Am I ready to make this commitment? Will it pay off?'

It's now January. Another holiday season has passed, and Sophia is bundled up on the couch relaxing with her husband, binge-watching the latest *Game of Thrones* season. Together, they discuss her conversation with Coronado University, and talk about her options. They're both young parents with what feels like very limited time in the day. Because she is so busy with work and life, Sophia is still most interested in learning more about flexible options like Coronado's online degree program.

Amplifying content to target more potential customers

Lead nurture (like the newsletter email Sophia received from Coronado University) is a great retargeting tactic. Because the school knows what pages Sophia already viewed on its site, it can put her in a predetermined workflow within its lead management software. This workflow might consist of several emails or pieces of unique content designed to put some positive pressure on Sophia to move forward. The school carefully ensures any messaging she receives is appropriate for her stage in the customer journey. Obviously, they don't want to send out welcome messages over and over again.

Consider the movie, Hitch. In the film, Will Smith is a relationship consultant that works exclusively with men to help them build meaningful relationships. During the movie, Hitch advises a client who's secured a date with a woman who is (in the client's eyes) out of his league.

Figure #76: Hitch (2005)

Hitch's advice: "When you're wondering what to say or how you look, just remember, she's already out with you. That means she said 'yes' when she could have said 'no.' That means she made a plan when she could have just blown you off."

"That means it's no longer your job to make her like you. It's your job not to mess it up."

- Hitch

This is also really good advice when it comes to effective lead nurture. Think about it. Sophia already signed up to receive Coronado University's emails. They don't want to mess it up by sending her the wrong content or inundating her with too many emails, too quickly. Like Coronado, marketers should take a measured approach and create workflows that support where prospects are in the customer journey with the intent of helping them take that next step. Marketo found that 96 percent of visitors who come to your website aren't ready to buy after their first interaction. With that in mind, we need to build relationships with individuals who have shown interest in our brand to push them to make a purchase down the road.

Continuing the theme of movie references, you might remember the popular quote from Field of Dreams, "If you build it, he will come." While that might be relevant for a bunch of baseball-playing ghosts, it's not necessarily the case when it comes to content. This is largely due to how we retain information online. Our brains are amazing filters. Jay Walker-Smith of Kantar Consulting says we're assaulted with more than 5,000 marketing and advertising messages every day. "We have to screen it out because we simply can't absorb that much information. We can't process that much data," he said.[52] "So, no surprise, consumers are reacting negatively to the kind of marketing blitz; the kind of super-saturation of advertising that they're exposed to on a daily basis," he continued in an interview with CBS News in 2006. That's right. He didn't say it yesterday — he said it twelve years ago. We're willing to bet you can go an entire day now without noticing a large percentage of the ads he was talking about.

Jerry Seinfeld, once said, "There is no such thing as an attention span. There is only the quality of what you are viewing. This whole idea of an attention span is, I think, a misnomer. People have an infinite attention span if you are entertaining them."

Another comedian, Steve Martin, offered a similar statement: "Be so good they can't ignore you."

---

52 https://www.cbsnews.com/news/cutting-through-advertising-clutter/

Because we're a distracted society, many of us multi-task and move from screen to screen throughout the day, chasing shiny objects that attract our attention (squirrel!). But Jerry and Steve have it right. Organizations can break through the clutter if they deliver content that's so good the audience can't possibly ignore it.

Using amplification to break through your audience's internal filters

If it weren't for our ability to filter out non-essential messages, we'd never get anything done. That's essentially what amplification — specifically paid media — is all about. Amplification is a much more proactive way to put those pieces of content to work, and have a sophisticated conversation that moves an audience through the customer journey. Brands aren't bringing their prospects back to the same landing page or sending them to their websites and hoping they find the way to a service or contact page. Without amplification, you're crossing your fingers and hoping people see your highest-converting content. Or, at the very least, hoping that you look better than any of the competition.

Content amplification aims at expanding the reach of content to target audiences when and where they need it most. When executed effectively, amplified content can reach a wider and more targeted audience than it would on its own. Think of the ads you see on Facebook, posts from someone you follow on LinkedIn or even tweets from an influencer you follow on Twitter. These are strategies of content amplification that are produced to put content in front of not only more people, but the right people.

When should content amplification be used to support the customer journey?

The customer journey is not linear. Sophia has visited the school's website on many occasions, and she's most likely been retargeted with other forms of content from competing universities throughout her months of research. This is important to note, because organizations most often put their focus, budget and resources on amplifying content that's catered to later stages of the journey, rather than earlier. From a strategic standpoint, only amplifying content or using paid media to target people in the decision stage is a common mistake — a strategy that often leaves a lot of potential revenue on the table.

Erik Solan, Vice President of Client Services & Strategy at Vertical Measures, positions a unique analogy for strategizing amplification earlier in the customer journey: "Have you ever been on Mill Avenue near ASU in Tempe, Arizona? You walk by a bar on a Saturday night, and there's people standing in front of each bar handing out fliers that basically beg, 'Please come in to our bar.' These people are hoping that because you're on Mill Avenue late on a Saturday night, because you're as close as you can get without actually walking in, you'll end up wandering in and buying a drink — or four."

Solan continues, "That always struck me. Why are you standing outside of your own bar? I'm already outside of the bar. If I liked what I saw, I would walk in. Right?"

"These little bar fliers act as the last-ditch effort to get me in for a two-for-one special, or whatever. But the amount of people that walked down that street, right in front of the bar, is possibly the smallest audience that bar could reach. Of course, in the bar's eyes, they think, "Well, those are the most likely to walk in and buy a drink," Solan explains.

"Yeah, you might land a 50 percent conversion rate if the offer is good enough. But for other verticals, where the buying cycle is longer, it's not smart. Why wouldn't you move the staff handing out fliers and put them one mile out from your bar? There might only be 100 people who walk right in front of the bar, but a thousand others down the road who might still be interested."

By appealing to a larger audience with a different offer, you avoid sitting in the lower funnel and simply waiting for people to show up. When you fill the upper stage of the funnel, and amplify your message earlier in the customer journey, you start to fill the middle of the funnel with more people that are asking questions with your product or service in mind. You increase the click-through rate and you increase the engagement rate so when next Saturday night rolls around, you might get 500 people walking by your bar instead of 100. Apply that to your own organization and the sheer number of online users, and you could be missing out on tens of thousands of potential customers.

This is an important distinction with amplification: As in Sophia's case, the paid media put in front of users has to be targeted and strategic to meet them wherever they are in the customer journey. At the beginning of her journey, Sophia's questions were very top-of-funnel. As she became more interested in pursuing her educational goal, her search terms get more specific. Coronado University's only chance at reaching Sophia during each stage was to develop a content amplification strategy that incorporated tactics to serve Sophia with the most relevant content when she was ready to receive it.

How was Sophia targeted so far in her journey?

For the sake of our story, we decided to focus on amplification later in the customer journey, but we could've moved this section to the first few chapters, back when Sophia was still in the awareness stage. Re-targeting Sophia most likely began when she first visited Coronado's website — and it all started with a cookie. We're not talking about the Girl Scout cookies hidden in her top desk-drawer at work — we're talking about a website cookie that can track Sophia's online activity within a specific browser.

A large amount of your audience will never provide a personal identifier voluntarily. That's just the nature of the digital conversation. Some people are very comfortable trading an email address or a phone number for information, while others will never share. For those who guard their personal information, brands can track behavior through an analytics program like Google Analytics (GA). Cookies allow you to understand your audience based on their behaviors, such as time on site, visits to a certain page or taking certain actions. With cookies, each person that comes to your site is uniquely tagged and their behavior is tracked.

Cookies can tell you:

- Where did your customers go on your site?
- How long did they spend there?
- What type of actions did they take?
- Did they return to the site later?
- How did they get to this site in the first place?
- What channel brought them there?
- Was it social? Was it a search? What type of search?
- Where were they located?
- What kind of device were they on?

All this information is contained in the cookie, including all behaviors before and after a user came to a brand's website. This might sound pretty straightforward, but if anything, there's too much information to digest. Brands often need an analytics expert to help decipher what parts of this data is worth using, such as proximity. If you have a brick-and-mortar location and a prospect is within 50 miles of your location versus another that's 500 miles away, you may want to put extra effort to amplify your content to the individual who's closer. The person who is 500 miles away may have 10 options between you and their location.

This data allows you to not only choose whom to target, but also choose whom to exclude. From here, you can choose how to spend your budget wisely so you're not investing on targeting everyone with your content. You could learn if the targeted audience looks engaged, if they spent more than two minutes on your website, if they went to three or more pages, if they ended on a program or a service-specific page, but they didn't fill out the form. This segmented audience, based solely on information provided from a standard cookie, should be put into a bucket of highly engaged audience that requires specific messaging.

Brands can follow each cookie to sites users visit after your own website, and place specific messaging on the next page they visit with a display ad that says, "Hey, we saw you were interested in this service, watch this video!" Or, "We saw that you didn't take action, so here's what you need to see in order to feel comfortable about buying from us." The actual copy should be more strategically worded, but you get the idea.

Using the data from your analytics, you can also learn more about users who do end up converting on your website. This data can provide useful information on how to accurately target other prospects with similar behaviors.

- Where do they come in?
- What pages do they visit?
- How long do they spend?
- What actions do they take?
- When do they convert?
- How long did the whole process take?
- Did it take seven days, 14, 45, 90?
- Were they on a mobile phone and then went to a desktop?
- What was the specific sequence of events?

After you've collected enough of this data, you can develop a model for more engaged audiences versus less engaged. For example, if someone went through the first steps that users typically do on your website, but then three days later never came back to where your users typically return, that might identify an area where you would start a specific email workflow or social retargeting campaign to call them back with a piece of content that might interest them most.

Keep in mind, you can get too specific. If you focus too much on specific behaviors, there might only be 50 people in that audience to retarget. Your audience buckets need to be broad enough so there's enough people to work with, but specific enough that you'll have a safe assumption that the blog posts, videos, infographics or whatever other types of content you show them will help this group move forward in their journey.

Content amplification
with owned media

To reach the largest possible audience, a unified amplification strategy across owned and paid approaches is crucial. Owned amplification refers to existing channel assets that your brand owns — any content over which a company has complete control. If someone like Sophia completes a search, comes to your website but doesn't convert, you should put them into a specific audience segment where a search campaign reacts to their next question in Google. You need to have precise copy for the next message. Whether it be a social ad, video ad, search ad or native ad, that initial copy must immediately grab that user's attention. Think of your website, branded blog posts, email newsletter, social posts and traditional media like printed direct mail. The more owned media channels that you have, the better, as long as the assets are maintained and kept relevant.

Social media channels

Owned social media channels are perfect tools to use when amplifying your site content. Organic and paid social media marketing strategies work together to increase the overall reach of your content and increase engagement with your brand.

Successful organizations target prospects using Facebook, Twitter, LinkedIn and Instagram, as these are the social channels where most people hang out online. Now remember, if you have more than three priorities, you have none. Rather than being mediocre at all social media channels, for example, Coronado University honed in on a couple that are used most frequently by prospective students. The university organically promotes content from its website and blog (examples of owned media) on certain social channels. Through these external channels, they attract new students and keep existing students engaged and well-informed. Where does your audience hang out online? Where do they spend time before or after visiting your website? The answer to this will help significantly when amplifying owned media on social channels.

Facebook is still the social giant, so we'll use it for a quick example. We know that Sophia uses Facebook to follow friends, create and join events, and also to follow influencers or brands that share her interests.

If your audience frequents Facebook like Sophia, you have the ability to create a workflow specifically for people who have been to a certain degree page, product page or service page but haven't converted yet.

Facebook looks at four things when ranking content on its feed:

- Who posted it?
- How did people engage with it?
- What type of post was it?
- When was it posted?

You want to be sure that when your site visitors go to Facebook later that evening to scroll through their feeds or catch up with friends and family (like Sophia), your next piece of inspirational content answers their needs and leads them toward a conversion. A few years ago, it was easier to place branded content in front of this social audience. But now, due to the latest Facebook algorithm update, being found organically in Facebook's feed is increasingly difficult. Facebook no longer gives brands the preferential treatment they used to.

"A third of the world uses social networks regularly."

- eMarketer

Businesses are seeing more than a 50 percent decline in their site visits from social when they only share content organically. Why? There are more than 1 billion websites online today, 60 million of which are marketing on Facebook. Facebook's organic content reach has been dramatically decreasing on the home page for users and being taken over by paid ad space. Now, only 6.5 percent of your followers see the organic content you post on average, with a staggering drop to just 2 percent if your page has more than 500,000 followers.[53]

---

53 https://www.cbsnews.com/news/cutting-through-advertising-clutter/

Content amplification
with earned media

Earned amplification occurs when an external publisher markets your brand through non-owned channels like social media, news coverage, or a review on YouTube. You should think of earned media like a big thumbs-ups for the great content that you have. If an influencer is willing to promote your content, it's likely because they believe in the product or service that you're offering, and audiences know that.

> "92% of people trust recommendations from individuals (even if they don't know them) over brands."
>
> - Nielsen

One of the chief characteristics of earned media is that you cannot control it. Marketers don't have much power over earned media — hey can't influence it in any way. It's happening because of direct experiences an audience has with your brand, positive or negative. Earned media typically comes in the form of reviews, testimonial videos, backlinks or other content produced organically on external channels.

Content amplification
with paid media

Paid amplification is a targeted, paid placement on behalf of your brand. A paid marketing strategy increases overall brand visibility by using existing audience-engagement metrics to direct targeted sponsored content. Sponsored placements allow you to choose when, where and how frequently your amplified content appears in front of prospective audiences, most likely through search and social media. Facebook and Google know everything about you — scary, we know — but this is good news for marketers. They can pay for ad space on search and social media platforms like Facebook, Twitter and Instagram so content is served to those who are most interested in becoming customers.

Influencer Posts

Influencer marketing is an approach to content amplification that centers on building relationships with key people or publications in your industry to produce and promote content for your brand. Effective influencer marketing amplifies content in channels where your target audience is already present and actively sharing ideas.

"81% of marketers who have used influencer marketing judged it to be effective."

— eMarketer

Influencer amplification should be thought of as an ongoing effort to connect industry experts with your prospects to shed a positive light on your brand. Engage in content co-creation between your organization and influencer and develop new contests and giveaways. Think of how Magellan University used influencer marketing at the beginning of our story. They might have lost Sophia's business due to a gap in their content, but for the most part, they had tweets, imagery, traditional advertisements, and more from influencers who helped promote their programs. This was, after all, what got Sophia started on her journey. The thought process behind using influencer posts is the ability to tap into another large following (owned mostly by the influencer) that your brand can use to get in front of more prospects.

Developing a winning
content amplification strategy

Sometimes people don't like to mention this, maybe because they're intimidated by the enormity of the organization, or because they rely on it for the wellness of their own businesses, but Google is simply an advertising company. Just like Facebook, and everyone else, they don't want you to get free traffic.

"Google makes approximately $100,000,000 in a day from AdWords."

— Search Engine Land

An organic approach will always be the backbone of a winning SEO strategy, but over the last decade (and even more so in the last few years), the re-engineering of the SERPs to blend ads with organic results continues to place emphasis on paid media. Sure, they want to provide the most relevant results for users, but they are also fine with those results being promoted behind paid amplification. Today, a business can pay to include more information on relevant searches, more local details (like hours and contact information), and pictures of its building or product, right there on Google.

Your audience is not scared to click an ad on the Google SERPs anymore. In fact, data shows many audiences are becoming more comfortable with clicking on those paid placements, rather than on the organic results. However, if you currently rank #1 for a search query, try this: Google that query on a mobile device. Are you even visible in the results page without scrolling?

"More than 50% of millennials use their mobile devices to research products."

- Hanover Research

It used to be that when you were visible, you were the answer. But now, users must scroll to even see the organic listings on mobile. And as we've illustrated throughout this book, most of your audience is using mobile to conduct their research throughout the entire customer journey. That's a large audience you might be missing out on if there's no investment or strategy for paid amplification. Erik Solan notes a common theme between successful and failing amplification strategies: "The battle needs to be won before that initial search even occurs, and that means amplifying content at the awareness stage, getting in front of that person before they even make the first query. So, when they do the query and see whether it's paid or organic they recognize you, the trust is already there, and then they click-through."

Today's digital marketing landscape means you're not going to achieve that true awareness from your audience unless you pay to get in front of them. You can't find that organic success in the awareness stage unless someone's already looking for your brand or specific product. Your top organic position in Google just might not be good enough anymore, and that's because brands are beginning "conquest campaigns" where they purchase the top ad space on your winning organic queries to steal that potential traffic. Your competition might be trying to push you down in the SERPs, and the only way you're going to get that visibility back is by knowing when to put budget behind amplification on certain queries. Sometimes we forget that paid search and organic search is still search – users are still asking the same question – but now there are two different ways to reach them and two different places to show up in the SERPs.

A common question we get is, "Should I bid on my brand terms?" And we've modified our answer over the last couple years. It's always yes, but for different reasons. Today we would start the answer with another question, "Does anyone see you as a competitor?" If someone sees you as a competitor, and they have a good paid amplification strategy, they'll immediately see when your brand no longer occupies the top result for your brand term. If you're not paying for your own brand terms, Google will happily take money from a competitor and rank them in position 1 for YOUR brand term, ahead of your organic ranking, right in front of your prospects' eyes.

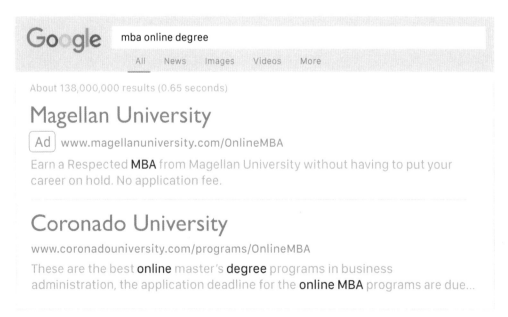

Figure #77: Coronado University ranks #1 organically, but Magellan owns the top paid position in the SERPs

They might be sneaking into that spot for pennies, because no one else is competing for the term. The term you could be owning organically and through paid might be one of the cheapest ones they could buy. And if your brand doesn't have a strategy to combat this, you may be losing a prospect that was very close to deciding on using your service or product. Unlike the increasingly limited control you have over the organic position in the SERPs, you could create a paid ad that expresses urgency and increases click-through rates. Who knows, you might even kick a competitor out of that top position, driving more traffic to some of your highest-converting pages.

We showed our client examples of branded queries their audience might use in search, and sure enough, they weren't in the top paid results; their competitors were. This competing brand had a nice, big fat ad on the top of the result page. On a desktop or laptop, a user could still see the client's organic listing, but on mobile (which is what their audience used most) you could only see their competitor. What kind of impression does that make? In a way, it looked like our client couldn't afford to show up for their own term. And it also made it look like they don't pay attention to their audience. How many tens of thousands of dollars could that be costing you?

For our client, this was a great real-world example of why putting paid amplification on their own brand terms directly impacted their ROI, but also why SEO and paid media must work together. It solidified their need to implement both paid and organic throughout the strategy, because in most circumstances, the click-through rate is close to double what it would be if just the organic listing is there.

Estimating ROI from your amplification efforts

Let's spend more time talking about getting a solid return on investment from paid amplification. Forget the formula where we promote a piece of content to an audience, we get them to the site, they buy something, and we know exactly what that product is worth. That's easy. To create a real estimate for paid amplification, let's use Coronado University as an example.

If it were trying to gain page views that result in more student enrollment, we would first ask:

- How long does someone stay on any given page?
- Do they end up graduating? If so, what's that rate?
- What's the cost of the program they're interested in?
- What revenue do you make on each student?

If you're paying $20 for every 1,000 page views, what's the lifetime value of those visits? Let's say the school makes $20,000 per student per semester. What does that average per month? How long does the average student stay enrolled? Let's pretend the school was able to obtain a 0.02 percent click-through rate in search. Using our formula above, if the school gets two clicks, each one costs $10. The school gets two people on a landing page and asks them both to fill out a form, but only one of the two provides an email address.

What did that email address cost? The $20 investment got the initial two clicks, but only one provided their email, so theoretically, it cost $20 to gain that contact. This email address goes into a lead nurture workflow. The school knows from previous measurement that 10 percent of email contacts entered into this workflow convert and enroll in a program. Another easy way to look at this: The school needs 10 emails to get one purchase. So, what do these ten emails cost the school? $200. And their ROI would be calculated by the lifetime value of their students (customers), but we will spare the details of that for the sake of your sanity. Obviously, if the close rate was that successful, universities would be investing a lot more than $20 for 1,000 page views, but you get the point.

You help start a relationship with your audience through amplification, and that should yield email or contact information for your organization. And, if you're using lead nurture effectively, a contact should convert into a paying customer. But you need certain details in order to estimate an ROI from your specific amplification efforts. You need to know order values or lifetime value, and you must track analytics to see how a user moves through your purchase process. The best digital strategies include amplification, content, and organic tactics working together. If a digital strategy does not include both organic content and amplification tactics, there will be gaps in your ability to get in front of the ideal audience.

It's like creating a staircase to your product, but with some steps missing. Some people will have long enough legs to reach the next step, but others will fall right through. And when they fall through, there will be another set of stairs right below, leading to someone else's product. That's digital marketing without amplification.

Sophia is retargeted
with more content

With so much engagement from Sophia, she's opened many options for Coronado University to amplify content targeted specifically for her. They've set cookies on her browser, know what pages she's visited on their site, know what content she's interested in and know what ads she's already consumed. This makes it easier for Coronado to reach her with the right content at the right time. She's almost completed her journey — it's up to the school to answer any final questions she may have to make that final decision.

Main Takeaways
& Action Steps

1

How can you use analytics (or change how you're using them) to better understand your customers?

2

Search a non-branded term related to your business from your mobile device. Where do you show up, if at all?

3

When in the customer journey would amplification make sense for your brand, and in which channels?

CHAPTER X
Sophia nears her decision

While browsing her Facebook feed, Sophia sees a retargeting ad video from Coronado University. She's already engaged with the university several times, consuming their content in different formats across multiple offline and online channels. The school has provided all the information she needs at this point, but Sophia (like the rest of us) needs some positive reinforcement to take that last step. To confirm she's going to make the right decision, she turns to Google search once again. This time, she remembers her conversation a few nights before with her husband. She searches for her trusted brand: "Coronado University Online vs Brick and Mortar Schools."

Coronado University Online vs Brick and Mortar Schools	🔍

online mba vs **mba**

online mba vs **executive mba**

online mba vs **on campus**

online mba vs part time mba

online mba vs **in person**

online mba vs **distance** mba

online mba vs **emba**

Figure #78: Google search for "Coronado University online vs brick and mortar school"

Remember, your prospects are evaluating you against your stiffest competition — you can't afford a content gap at this stage. For important decisions, conversion often comes down to having answers to just a few critical questions. Make sure you're communicating with your sales department and customer service department (if available) to find out all the questions they're fielding on a regular basis, so you can publish content with the answers your prospects need. We talked about this in chapter 3, and we'll discuss it further in this chapter as we highlight how to qualify leads.

The decision stage of the customer journey is where it gets really interesting for digital marketers. The prospect has engaged with content on your site and, in many cases, also on different paid and organic channels. Now, you must reinforce your company's value and place lower-funnel content in front of the prospect to continue your online conversation.

At Vertical Measures, we sometimes see companies that only focus on lower-funnel content and miss prospects in the awareness and consideration stages. We also see companies that don't have enough decision-focused content and fail by regurgitating the same content that they've delivered before. Your prospects expect a level of sophistication at this point. They want to know you're listening.

> **"91% of consumers are more likely to shop with brands that recognize and remember them, and provide relevant offers and recommendations."**
>
> – Accenture Interactive

If your business is service-focused, you can include interactive content, videos and user-generated content such as testimonials and reviews in this stage. If you're product-based and focused on sales, you can include your product lines, product pages, plus-one offers, free trials and similar content.

Types of content that are perfect for the decision stage

Product pages

Product pages are a very important part of decision-focused content. Remember, the potential lead wants all the information they can get prior to talking with a salesperson, so you must have complete descriptions of your products and services. When you answer questions and educate, you're taking the place of cold calls from your sales team. Your potential customer should be so well informed that they have very few, if any, questions prior to engaging in direct communication with your company.

It's important to remember that many manufacturers provide product content to their distributors and the distributor publishes the content verbatim. This is what Google refers to as duplicate content. Neither the manufacturer nor the distributor will derive any benefit in rankings by publishing duplicate content, and in some cases may lose ranking because of it. You should have unique content on your website in order to have the best chance of ranking. One way to approach this is to create two versions of your content and publish one set of unique content on your site and make the other version available to any distributors or affiliates.

Pricing tables

Pricing tables are a good way to display your various levels of service and products. There's a science behind presenting the information, and you can set hypotheses for conversion rate optimization based on your layout, colors and emphasis on a particular level or price.

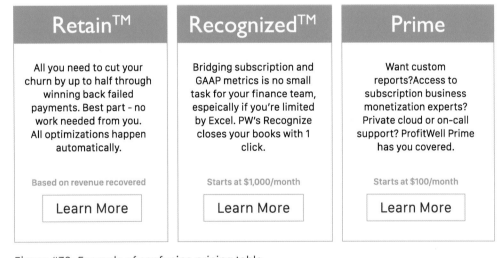

Figure #79: Example of confusing pricing table
(Source: https://neilpatel.com/blog/pricing-page-that-converts/

Emphasizing a price or plan can immediately draw the user's attention and highlight your best offer or your highest-converting offer. A simple, clean design works best. Don't use generalized information that doesn't clearly differentiate service or product pricing levels. Most pricing tables are designed with a horizontal format so it's easier to compare choices.

Here are some quick tips:

- Communicate essential information and nothing else. Often, businesses try to include too much information in the table. Make the pricing data easily scannable so visitors can get the information they need quickly.
- Call out the differences in your pricing plans, not the similarities. An example might be to put the distinctive features of each plan at the top of the table and the common features at the bottom.
- Make the actual prices stand out. After all, that is why the user is on this page. Design can help draw the eye with intentional use of colors, fonts and icons.
- Reduce clutter. Limit the number of visuals on the page. A clear and well-organized pricing page will convert better than one with too many visual distractions.
- Make strong visual distinctions between the various plans or pricing options. You don't need to tell users to make the comparison — they will do it all on their own.

Free trials

If you have a service business, free trials can draw the user into using your tools. Once engaged, they have the opportunity to see how the services apply to them and how they feel about the commitment. The free trial should be designed in a way that the next logical step for the user is to sign up for the paid version.

Figure #80: Example of service offerings that include a free trial

Trials with limited functionality do not convert as well as letting the user have full access to all the tools for a limited time. You want the user to see the full value of your service and be so engaged that they sign-up without hestitation.

Testimonials

People want to know how others have used your products and their results. Even for small purchases, testimonials can be powerful. Testimonials that confirm others have bought and had a good experience with their purchase are great closing tool. There are customers out there that have experienced a dramatic and positive impact on their business or lives because of your product or service. The key is to find them and entice them to share their experiences.

"Any business that has delighted customers has a sales force out there that you don't have to pay. You don't see them, but they are talking to people all the time."

- Warren Buffet

Testimonials fall into two buckets

- **Qualitative:** Content focuses on emotional satisfaction and appeals to the reader or viewer on a personal level.
- **Quantitative:** Content focuses on delivery, product or service features and the speed or quality of your impact on the reviewer.

What makes a good testimonial

- **Short:** It gets to the point immediately.
- **Focused:** It defines what made an impact on the customer and how.
- **Authentic:** It comes from the customer and feels truthful and real.

Finally, you need to make it as easy as possible for the reviewer to deliver the testimonial, whether through text or video. Provide a sample text and offer the reviewer complete control to edit as they see fit. Create a process that can be followed. Don't go about this in an ad hoc fashion. Ask specific questions about how your product or service met or exceeded their needs, and shoot a video of happy customers answering the questions. If you have a studio or if your reviewer has an office, you can shoot a more professional-looking video, but really, users today are willing to accept lower-quality video testimonials as long as they're genuine. If video isn't an option, publish a photo of your happy customer. As we've noted before, the human-element results in higher conversions.

Reviews

Just like testimonials, reviews give the prospect more information about your services, products and company and the interaction they had with you. Positive reviews can help close the sale as well.

"90% of consumers read online reviews before visiting a business."

- BrightLocal

In order to solicit reviews, you may create comment cards or surveys and ask for feedback on any potential negative encounters. As in testimonials, it's best to get feedback immediately, especially on positive interactions. Customers are more likely to post bad reviews than good. We'll touch on this more later in the book.

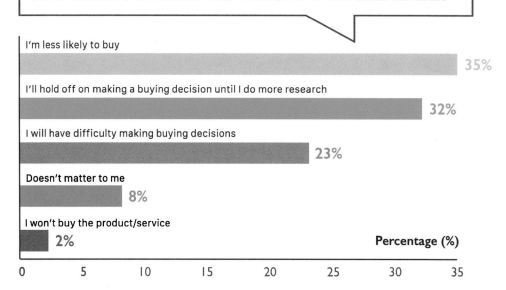

Figure #81: The importance of customer reviews (Source: SocialMediaToday)

Free consultations

Free consultations are a powerful tool, especially for service businesses. Once you connect with the potential customer and speak with them directly, you can ask questions to position your services that will solve their problems. In the decision stage, the prospect is more likely to ask for a consultation. They've read your content and trusted you enough to take this step.

We often provide free consultations. For us, it showcases our abilities and gives us one more chance to persuade a potential client. During the consultation, we're able to show how we think and how we would interact with clients to see if we're a good fit.

Coupons, discounts and upsells

Use coupons and discounts as quick motivations to buy now. Make sure to place time limits on the discounts so the lead will lose the opportunity if they don't act now. Discounts and coupons are considered the top-ranking tactic for driving loyalty, with 61 percent of consumers saying they use them, according to Expedia Affiliate Network.[54] Adding information on additional products in this stage can help you increase your average order value, or AOV. Amazon does a great job of this.

Frequently bought together

Total price: $325.86

Add all three to Cart

Add all three to List

☑ This item: Apple iPad (WiFi, 32GB) - Space Gray (Latest Model) $298.88
☑ [2 Pack] iPad 9.7 in (2018/2017) $11.99
☑ iPad 9.7 2018/2017 Casem Lightweight Smart Case Trifold Stand $14.99

Figure #82: "Frequently bought together" example

54 https://globenewswire.com/news-release/2018/04/09/1466757/0/en/Driving-loyalty-through-customer-experience-is-the-future-for-travel-says-research-survey-by-Expedia-Affiliate-Network-and-Points.html

Versus content (comparisons)

Potential customers want to know how your product or services stack up to the competition. We find comparisons are often a gap in decision-stage content, because clients are afraid to feature the competition at all on their own website. The business "doesn't feel comfortable" about including such information on the site because it could steer potential prospects away. To this, we tell them to remember that if they publish the comparison content, the lead is reading about it on their website. With proper calls-to-action and positive user experience, you can lead them to a sale. If you don't publish this kind of comparative content, your competitor will and you could potentially lose the customer.

Remember poor Magellan University?
That's okay, Sophia probably won't, either.

In our story, Sophia made a search comparing brick-and-mortar vs online classes. She could also make a comparison search based on the brand. For example, she might search: Coronado University vs UCLA. This is the type of information your potential customer is searching for in Google, and you need to have a piece of that lower-funnel, high-converting, decision-stage content ready for them.

Unleash the full power of
"smarketing"

The funnel narrows even more as Sophia is eliminating final possibilities. As we've known for awhile now, Coronado University is the best decision for Sophia, specifically its online MBA in Marketing program. And like the best companies in the world, our humble university in Southern California has an efficient process with sales and marketing departments working together. HubSpot calls it Smarketing.

"The term "Smarketing" refers to alignment between your sales and marketing teams created through frequent and direct communication between the two."

- HubSpot

The goal is to have measurable goals that each team agrees to hit so there's mutual accountability. For instance, marketing might have a mutually agreed upon leads SLA (service level agreement) to achieve, and sales must agree to follow up with a certain amount of those leads. Smarketing goals should be made together and re-evaluated every month or at least quarterly to identify opportunities for improvement on both teams.[55]

Marketing Qualified Leads (MQLs)

These are leads more likely to become a customer based on the interaction they've had with your brand online. Data is gathered through closed-loop analytics to determine the inherent value of the lead. These closed-loop analytics are actually a collaboration, with your sales team providing quantitative and qualitative data that involves the entire customer journey. So, instead of guessing what prospects are most likely to buy, you're aligning your sales and marketing departments based on what known activities and engagement are most likely to end up converting to a sale. (See more about this in Chapter 11 where we highlight attribution modeling).

Setting parameters for MQLs needs to be a collaborative effort. Setting too tight a definition could result in not providing enough leads to the sales team, while having too loose a definition could result in wasted time and resources. It takes some negotiation to arrive at your company's definition, and over time, it should be reviewed and updated based on measured results. These metrics or goals might include the amount of traffic your site receives, and the number of leads generated. We find that quarterly meetings allow us enough time to gather good data and make necessary changes. One way to define your MQL is to work backward from a conversion:

- Who are your customers?
- How many touchpoints did they have prior to a sale?
- What are their demographics of your customers or their firms?
- What is the sales cycle timeline and other data you can collect from current customers?
- What is the most likely path a new customer will take, and where is the handoff to sales?

55 https://blog.hubspot.com/marketing/definition-smarketing-under-100-words

It's important to remember that the MQL isn't ready to buy, but they are paying attention to your proposed solutions and the products or services you provide. Definitions for MQLs don't need to be over-complicated for your team. They could be simple, like the prospect has viewed two blog posts and downloaded at least one piece of content from your website. When the prospect meets your defined criteria, they become an MQL.

The prospect:

- Demonstrated some level of engagement on the website
- Indicated they have a need by having downloaded content or filled out a form
- Aligns well with your best personas
- Fulfills the requisite qualifiers for their firms

As the marketing department meets with sales, you can develop both your MQLs and SQLs.

Sales Qualified Leads (SQLs)

SQLs are leads that passed marketing's muster and your sales team's criteria. The lead is now moving from the consideration stage into the decision stage of your customer journey. The SQL continues to engage with your website and increase the number of touchpoints with your content. And, as our familiar trend continues, the key is to provide content that solves their problem and moves them toward making a purchase decision. Some of the criteria for an SQL is the same as an MQL, but the number and possibly the frequency of interactions with your content has increased.

An SQL typically:

- Came to your site from a channel that converts well
- Continued consumption of content on your site
- Signed up for a newsletter and is actually opening it
- Downloaded multiple pieces of content
- Visited or revisited your pricing page
- Has a title or role that identifies them as a decision maker

Because there are no set criteria to help define MQLs and SQLs, your sales and marketing departments must communicate with each other on a regular basis to better understand the quality of the visitors coming to your website. Only then will you know the best content to produce and the best channels to use in order to convert them into a paying customers. There are many programs that help with this process, including HubSpot, which is the platform we use at Vertical Measures. Other platforms include Salesforce, Marketo, Pardot, Infusionsoft and many others.

How to prioritize resources
to respond to your best leads

Not everyone who comes to your site, downloads content and engages with your brand is of equal value. A good example of this is our own website, www.verticalmeasures.com. We publish a great quantity of information around all things digital marketing. As such, we know many other digital marketing companies consume our content. We also know they are not good prospects for us. They're coming to the site to learn more about digital marketing and to stay current on trends and techniques, and we love that. We continue to communicate with them and build relationships, but we know they are a low priority as a potential sale for our related services. And for that, we use data to better understand who the best prospects are for our company. Here's how you can do it:

As potential customers/clients move through the customer journey, you can qualify them based on the content they consume and the overall interaction they have with your site. Knowing their particular interactions with your content can allow you to rank and prioritize who and how you will continue to engage. For example, a user might review your pricing page, leave, and then come back several times over the course of days or weeks. In this case, the user is showing a sense of urgency and in most cases will be a much better lead than someone who bounces after reviewing one page.

You can start with demographic information that supports your personas, and then use firmographic information that could include, name, title (role), company, annual company revenue and other information. All of this info can help you better understand the exact contact and the quality of the lead for your company. This qualitative data can come from your sales team and from your customer services team. Painting a picture with both qualitative and quantitative data will give you the most complete information for lead scoring.

"Without data, you're just another person with an opinion."

- W. Edwards Deming

There's certain criteria you can use to qualify a lead. One popular method is known as BANT, which was developed by IBM.

BANT is an acronym for:

Budget
The prospect has the budget to engage with you.

Authority
The prospect has the authority to make a decision or can strongly influence another

Need
They have a definite or perceived need or problem you can help them solve.

Timeline
They have a sense of urgency.

Figure #83: BANT

This is a popular framework, but may not satisfy your unique product or service. The key is to consider any additional characteristics revealed by the prospect that make them qualified buyers and show intent to move forward toward a decision. You will use this information as you develop your sales qualification lead definition.

The importance of optimizing
for mobile and tablet devices

As Coronado University reengages with Sophia, they're keen to focus on mobile and tablet devices. They're seeing a continued increase in traffic from these devices and notice that their desktop traffic is declining. Diving closer into their Google Analytics, they also note that organic clicks on mobile devices are declining. Now, we know what you're thinking, "I thought you literally just said their traffic was increasing on mobile. Have I been reading this book too long or am I taking crazy pills?" The answer is yes, probably, to both questions. But the difference between mobile traffic and organic clicks is an important one, so let's continue. Coronado's overall traffic may be increasing from mobile, but the percentage of clicks on organic mobile is declining based on the fact that paid ads are pushing all their organic listings below the fold on mobile devices.

It's because of Google's search results page layout. Organic listings do not show in most cases above the fold, and users need to scroll down to actually see any organic listings. A recent study by SparkToro and Jumpshot shows how dramatic the drop in organic clicks is on mobile devices.[56]

Mobile search click-through
Organic & Paid CTR - November 2015 - February 2018

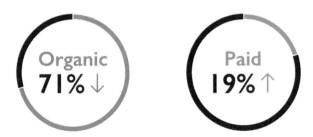

Figure #84: Mobile search click-through (Source: SparkToro)

Are you experiencing similar issues? You might also note that overall clicks from searches are declining. This might be due to Google's answer box answering many questions within results pages themselves, eliminating the need for another click. We see this trend continuing and growing.

---

56 https://sparktoro.com/blog/new-data-how-googles-organic-paid-ctrs-have-changed-2015-2018/

Contacting a lead: a case study

Have you ever experienced an overzealous smarketing team? Where once you traded your personal information for content, the company was overly aggressive in contacting you? We all want our businesses to succeed and generally speaking, making a quick connection with a lead results in higher close ratios. That's not always true, however, as this summary of one of our case studies proves.

Our client was immediately calling anyone that downloaded a piece of their content. Can you imagine that? You download some white-paper and while you're still reading the opening paragraph a sales rep calls your cell phone five minutes later? Needless to say, their results in closing was a dismal zero percent. We scheduled a meeting with both their sales and marketing teams to share data and anecdotal information (quantitative and qualitative).

In our discussions, we determined:

- A one-time download/engagement had the lowest close percentage
- A two-time download/engagement had a higher close percentage
- A three-plus download/engagement had the highest close percentage

Based on this shared information, the sales department changed its priorities to focus on the 3x engagement leads. Their close ratio went up dramatically. It makes sense, right? These leads were much more engaged and had interacted more with the content on the site.

How do you know when is the right time to call? You could do it like some companies and include the following on your lead form: "Would you like to be contacted by one of our consultants?" This way, the prospect self-identifies that they are ready to engage. Or, you could be annoying and have a pop-up launched within five seconds of the first visit to the site.

Our short-but-sweet case study illustrates the need for analyzing data on how users engage with your brand in all digital channels, including your website. From there you must determine their value and segment them by creating MQLs and SQLs.

Main Takeaways
& Action Steps

1

What types of content would be valuable to prospects in the decision stage of your customer journey?

2

What characteristics define a Marketing Qualified Lead (MQL) for your business?

3

What characteristics define a Sales Qualified Lead (SQL) for your business?

CHAPTER XI
Attributing value to multiple marketing channels

As we've tried to represent with Sophia, your prospects may often take a circuitous route on the way to making a purchase decision. When you use multiple channels for your marketing, you must understand what's working and what isn't and continually improve your strategy based on those findings. With today's sophisticated automation tools, you should be able to monitor the data that will help you make better decisions.

One in four millennials share online shopping content on their social networks – which is a rate of nearly four times the average user. It's useful, too. Their content generates 18 more clickbacks per link, 30 percent above average.[57] Where do you place value on the channels that assisted in making the sale? That is, how do you assign attribution values to each interaction?

Facebook 15% Radio 5% LinkedIn 5% Search 15%

TV 10% Local 15% Your Site 20% In-Store 20%

Attribution is the science of assigning values of a sale to the touchpoints that influenced the sale during the customer journey. These touchpoints can cover a wide range of interactions and can be both online and offline, which allows you to take a much more holistic view of your marketing efforts.

57 https://www.adweek.com/digital/millennials-hugely-influential-among-peers-social-media/ce

The goal is to determine the value of each touchpoint to help decide if you should spend more or less or stop that channel/activity in your future marketing efforts. It allows you to make financially informed decisions for adjusting your marketing efforts.

Too many companies today rely on the same marketing channels they've used in the past (read: traditional marketing). Because they have a history with that channel, along with relationships with their sales representatives, they continue to do what they've always done without really understanding the value particular media or channels bring to the sales equation. The impact offline channels have on the online purchase has dropped off significantly in the past few years.

"[Marketers] continue to struggle to prove the ROI of their media plans, especially with their shift toward truly integrated cross-channel campaign strategies. These require a keen understanding of audience profiles, media engagement, attribution, sales lift and efficiency. Understanding engagement, influence and attribution by channel is not easy and is most challenging for traditional media that does not provide the engagement visibility afforded by digital channels."

- Chris Tingle, CMO Valassis

By assigning value, budget decisions can be made, moving money from one marketing channel to another. With this information, you can justify a current spend or make an argument to move dollars to another channel. Without this information, you're just guessing on what's actually contributing to your sale and potentially spending your hard-earned marketing dollars on something that may be very ineffective.

As UCLA marketing professor and MarketShare co-founder Dominique Hanssens instructs, "Knowing what to focus on — the signal rather than the noise — is a critical part of the process. To accurately model their businesses, companies must collect data across five broad categories: market conditions, competitive activities, marketing actions, consumer response, and business outcomes."

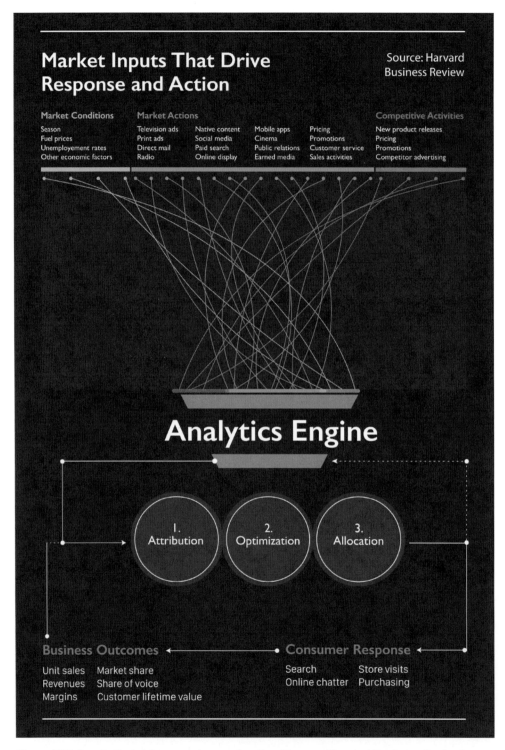

Figure #86: Inputs that drive response and action (Source: Harvard Business Review)

This image represents many of the inputs that can drive response and action. Where would you assign the most value? Where would you spend more or less? Why consider assigning attribution values? Take this scenario from Google as an example:

"A customer finds your site by clicking one of your Google Ads. She returns one week later by clicking over from a social network. That same day, she comes back a third time via one of your email campaigns, and a few hours later, she returns again directly and makes a purchase."[58]

If this were your business, would you like to know what assisted in the ultimate sale and where the most weight or impact came from? The above example is pretty simplistic, but what if you have a product or service with a long sales cycle? The user may do all the above, plus download a white paper on your site, take an interactive quiz on your site and interact with a post on LinkedIn. Without identifying what assisted in the sale and the relative value of each assist, you will never be able to determine the true ROI of your efforts. By determining attribution, you'll be able to argue your case to management to get more funds for the specific tactics that have the biggest impact on sales.

Assigning attribution can help:

- Identify inefficient spending
- Identify under-invested keywords
- Guide you to make smart changes in the channels you choose
- Show you where to spend more or less based on hard data

Types of attribution

If you're struggling to wrap your head around proper attribution for your company, out-of-the-box attribution modeling tools like Google Analytics can help you get started. Be warned, however, that these tools have default values that may or may not apply to your specific customer journey. You will, in most cases, need to edit your account to make it truly valuable for your team.

---

58 https://support.google.com/analytics/answer/1662518?hl=en

Some metrics to consider:

First Click:

Gives 100 percent of the value to the channel that brought the prospect to your website and disregards all other channels and touchpoints.

Last Click:

Gives 100 percent of the value to the channel that closed the prospect to become a lead or a customer based on your marketing goals.

Last AdWords Click:

Gives 100 percent of the attribution to your paid AdWords campaign.

Multi-touch or linear attribution allows you to assign values proportionally across all channels and devices both online and offline. Most marketers will give equal weight to each touchpoint when first setting this up. You'll need to assess the percentages as you analyze data and further measure the overall value of each touchpoint. The simplest and easiest way to assign value is to use Google Analytics. In order to do that, it must be linked to your Google Search Console and your AdWords accounts. Once you sync the three accounts, you can easily assign attribution for your campaign. In addition, you can assign revenue values to determine which channels are the most valuable to your sales. Again, once you can see the value of a channel, you can decide to do more or less in that particular channel.

As marketers, we're using both traditional and digital channels. We know they can both be beneficial to the end result — a sale. Remember, radio did not kill print, nor did TV kill radio. Each of these innovations did not kill the previous channels. There has been an impact on the efficiencies of traditional media, but if you can assign attribution to the various mediums, you'll better understand the impact and value they have on assisting the sale. This association of traditional and new media will continue to evolve as new platforms are introduced and disintermediation continues to impact the traditional channels.

Sophia enrolls in Coronado University's **online MBA program**

Sophia has made her decision. Get ready for this Shyamalan-of-all twists: She's enrolling at Coronado University. The marketing and sales departments at the university were working together to complete the customer journey, supported by strategy, content, promotion and measurement. Their content answered Sophia's questions at each stage, informed her about her choices and gained her trust.

But even though Sophia has made her decision, it's not over yet. Coronado's team will now continue to follow up with her in hopes she'll become an advocate for the university and possibly make her own testimonial video.

Main Takeaways
& Action Steps

1

How many touchpoints could your customers encounter online before making a purchase decision?

2

Which channels or content types do you think add the most value for a consumer on their way to a sale?

3

Based on the above, which channels or content types would be important to track in your attribution models?

CHAPTER XII
Sophia creates her own video testimonial

Sophia has now been enrolled at Coronado University for several months. She completed her customer journey through the decision stage, and now there's only one step left — to become an advocate for the Coronado University brand. This is a much-neglected stage of the journey, which is unfortunate, because it's also one of the most important. Continued engagement with current customers can help you with retention and provides the opportunity to prolong the relationship between loyal customers and your marketing department.

As your customer progresses through the customer journey, you build a relationship through your online content, offline and direct contact, along with your great products or services. In fact, at its core, the customer journey is about building this relationship. Until the internet, the only real way to become an advocate for a brand was through word-of-mouth. Now, every customer can let the world know about their experience with you through their digital bullhorn.

As we mentioned previously in this book, testimonials are an invaluable form of content for the decision and advocacy stage of the customer journey. Testimonials help prospects validate their impending purchases and make them feel more comfortable about decisions that might involve significant risk, involve large commitments of time or money or alter the course of their lives. In her journey to become a student, Sophia relied on both reviews and testimonials in order to make her feel comfortable enough to continue her education.

At this point, she's part of Coronado University's owned audience, which allows their marketing department to reach out to her with lead nurture email workflows. She's in a current workflow that solicits new students to create video testimonials.

Sophia!

Sophia! We're very happy to have such a high-performing member of the **Coronado University** family. We know your path is unique, and your story can inspire other young professionals to reach their potential -- just like you! We would like you to participate in producing a simple testimonial video describing your experience at Coronado University and how it has impacted your life. If you would like to help, please follow the button below.

Sincerely,

Pat MaGooch, Senior Director,
Coronado University

FILM YOUR VIDEO

Figure #87: Coronado University email enticing Sophia for video testimonail

This new email made her think about similar testimonials she watched in previous stages of her journey, where existing students talked about having the same doubts, challenges and issues that ran through Sophia's mind as she was deciding what to do. Reflecting on her current experience with the school, she's really excited about her professors, the online curriculum and the initial success she's enjoying. This fulfillment gives her the confidence and comfort level to share her own feelings about Coronado University.

You might already have been able to guess this, but testimonials are typically more powerful in video form. Not only do they add a personal element that resonates better with audiences, they're also easier to create (or ask others to produce). As we will cover in this chapter, you don't need high-quality production equipment to create effective video content these day – especially for simple testimonials.

Sophia's already been sharing her experiences with family and friends, so she's relatively comfortable with sharing those stories in the video. All she really has to do is repeat what she's already excitedly shared with her peers in front of a smartphone camera. Luckily for Coronado University, they've created such a positive experience for her, Sophia's enthusiasm about her journey and the new challenges she faces will naturally translate onto video.

Like Sophia, encouraging your current customers to become evangelists is an important advocacy tactic. They're already enthusiastic about your product or service and it's a matter of giving them a process to accommodate the creation of content. Video can create emotion and move the viewer to take action.

Why is video so powerful?

Video marketing is becoming increasingly important in all stages of the customer journey. We've decided to highlight it later in the book to align with Sophia's story, but you should be looking at using video at all stages to connect with your audience. Prospects want to know how a decision by another customer worked out, and video is a great way to quickly let them know. According to HubSpot, more than 90 percent of digital marketers are already using video as part of their digital marketing strategy.[59]

"More than 50% of internet users looked for videos related to a product or service before visiting a store."

- Think with Google

According to a study done by Vidyard Video, "Businesses are increasing their investments in both in-house and outsourced video content to help serve the growing demand for video throughout the customer lifecycle."[60]

---

59 https://blog.hubspot.com/marketing/video-marketing-statistics
60 https://www.vidyard.com/business-video-benchmarks/

There is a common misconception that video marketing is costly and difficult. It can be, depending on the sophistication and focus of your video. It can also be practical and inexpensive, and it has the ability to produce a great ROI. One of the most successful and inexpensive examples of video is the famous Dollar Shave Club YouTube video.[61] The video cost $4,500 to produce. Within 48 hours of publication it generated more than 12,000 orders. The video now has more than 25 million views, and it helped launch a billion-dollar company. (Unilever just purchased Dollar Shave Club for $1 billion.)[62]

DollarShaveClub.com - Our Blades Are F***ing Great

25,570,631 views

👍 122K 👎 2.4K ➡

Figure #88: Dollar Shave Club YouTube video (Source: Dollar Shave Club)

The viral success of this video is certainly an anomaly, but it does demonstrate that one inexpensive video can have a huge impact and ROI. If you watch the 93-second video, you'll learn about the company's products, philosophy, pricing and how to buy their product. It's a great testament to how video can tell your brand story in just a minute and half.

---

61 https://www.youtube.com/watch?v=ZUG9qYTJMsl

62 https://www.bloomberg.com/news/articles/2016-07-20/why-unilever-really-bought-dollar-shave-club

Are you using video in your digital marketing? If not, you're falling behind your competition. More video is uploaded in 30 days than the major U.S. TV networks have created in the past 30 years, and one-third of online activity is spent watching video.[63] Because video is so easy to consume, it's outpacing other forms of content marketing when it comes to creating relationships between businesses and their prospects and customers. Smart marketers are integrating video into every stage of the customer journey, on both the organic and paid advertising sides. As they deploy more video, companies see an increase in traffic, leads, conversions, sales, customer loyalty and referrals.

An engaging video can hold your prospects' attention, move them emotionally and inspire them to take action. It has the ability to train, entertain, influence, arouse intense feelings and convert like no other form of communication. Video produces an emotional shortcut to the brain and has the power to move someone to take action. In fact, viewers retain 95 percent of a message in a video compared to only 10 percent when reading it in text.[64] Video is able to engage the user on a much deeper level than any other form of communication.

"Video is projected to represent more than 80% of all web traffic by 2021."

- Cisco Visual Networking Index

Video engages the viewer on two levels, visually and aurally. Its multisensory nature makes video more impactful than text or still images. It's much easier to recall a message when two senses are engaged. A study by Comscore found that a website visitor will stay on a site two minutes longer when they watch a video. Adding video to email also helps with engagement — Forrester reports that including video in an email increases the click-through rate by 200 to 300 percent.[65]

---

63 https://www.wordstream.com/blog/ws/2017/03/08/video-marketing-statistics
64 https://www.insivia.com/27-video-stats-2017/
65 https://visual.ly/community/infographic/technology/online-video-consumption-numbers

Video also encourages social shares, which allows you to reach even more potential customers. In a survey conducted by Wyzowl, 76 percent of respondents said they would share a branded video if it was deemed entertaining.[66] You can increase traffic to your website by publishing video through your social media networks. Users on social media are constantly scanning their feeds, and video can attract their attention more easily than a wall of text. Once they view your content on their favorite social media channels, they can share it with their friends, potentially growing your reach exponentially. You can post organically or use video in social media advertising. Either way, it has the power to increase your reach and engagement.

On top of these benefits, you can also improve your website's SEO by adding video to landing pages and embedding it on content pages. Video illustrates to search engines that you have quality content and a robust media mix, which in turn sends trust signals that you have customer-aware conten on your site. Search engines include video as a ranking factor, and we believe they will continue to do so.

Optimizing video is just like optimizing images. You must name the file using priority keywords, include meta elements (alt text, title tags) that accurately describe the content and write a compelling title.

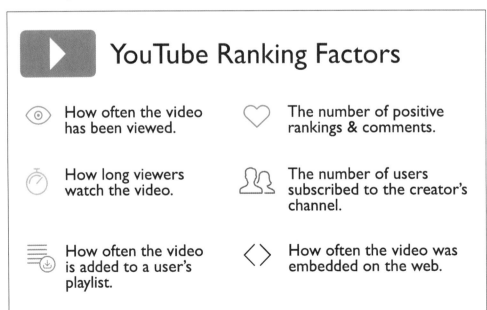

YouTube Ranking Factors

- How often the video has been viewed.
- How long viewers watch the video.
- How often the video is added to a user's playlist.
- The number of positive rankings & comments.
- The number of users subscribed to the creator's channel.
- How often the video was embedded on the web.

Figure #89: YouTube ranking factors

66 https://www.wyzowl.com/video-marketing-statistics-2016/

Adding a description or transcript of the video will also help with rankings. Transcripts improve "findability" and add further support for keyword and topic searches.

We suggest transcribing your video for two reasons:

1. To give more meat to the search engines, providing more opportunities to rank for the keywords within the video.

2. Transcription is best for the user. If they miss something in the video they can easily scan the text to find what they missed.

Use an embedded-video thumbnail wherever the video is located on your site to ensure it doesn't slow down your page-load speed. By using an embedded-video thumbnail, the video won't load until the user hits the play button. When the user clicks the play button, the image is replaced with the video player. You can also host your videos on various distribution channels instead of your site, such as YouTube or Vimeo. As a search engine, YouTube ranks second only to Google (its parent company) for overall internet traffic. By hosting on YouTube, you won't slow down your page-load speed, and additional exposure from the hosting site can lead to more eyes on your content. If you host videos externally, make sure to tag and categorize them and include a relevant link back to your site in the video description so the viewer can easily navigate to your owned channels.

There's a constant debate as to whether you should host video on YouTube or on your own site. The considerations for not hosting on YouTube are a slower page-load speed on your site and reduced opportunity for viewing traffic. The upside to hosting on your site is that any links to your video will be to your domain, not on YouTube. That choice is for you to make based on your specific marketing goals, but we typically recommend hosting on YouTube.

Whether they're hosted on your domain or YouTube, great videos can earn you links from other relevant domains. In fact, websites with video attract 300 percent more inbound links than those without.[67]

---

67 http://blog.visme.co/visual-seo-strategies/

Take our previous example on the Dollar Shave Club. A recent review of their backlink portfolio shows they have approximately 16,000 backlinks, many of them generated by the publication of their initial video. Again, don't expect to hit a home run every time you publish a video. This example is just to show you that you can earn links from a well-crafted video.

"Blog posts incorporating video attract three times as many inbound links as blog posts without video."

– Moz

Types of video content
that generate the best results

Your digital marketing strategy and goals should direct the type of video that your team creates. Like all content, video should be directed at your personas and align with these established goals. Don't create video just to create video – weave it into your overall marketing plans with purpose. Your video content should explicitly map to your customer journey with the focus on turning your viewers into paying customers. As marketers, we can create video with relative ease and for minimum expense.

But for maximum effectiveness, we must bake it into our overall strategy.

- What type of video will we create?
- What content topics will it cover?
- What stage of the customer journey will it focus on?
- What next steps will we want the viewer to take?
- What do we expect to see in terms of ROI for our time, trouble and effort?

"Video is like pizza — even when it's bad, it's still pretty good."

– DreamGrow

A strategy will also help you identify your resource needs and budget requirements. Remember, your video doesn't have to be studio quality every time, although there are a few types where you need to have professional production in order to show your brand in a quality setting.

Product videos

This is one of the most popular video types. They allow you to show your product or service and essentially take the place of a salesperson. It's like having a 24/7 representative for your brand that never takes vacation. Chances are, you already have all the information you need to storyboard product videos. It's like taking your sales sheets, product brochures and other marketing materials and creating a video using all that information. Product videos make for powerful closing tools, as 52 percent of consumers say that watching a video made them feel more confident about moving ahead to make a purchase.[68]

Figure #90: Apple Product Video (Source: Apple Video)

---

68 http://chittlesoft.com/blog/why-you-should-invest-in-good-about-us-videos/

Explainer videos

Not every business has a product to sell and for these businesses, explainer videos take the place of product videos. The intent of this type of video is to clearly explain a business' service or product in a clear and engaging way.

An explainer video takes the place of a wall of text explaining what you do. Explainer videos make it easy for the user to learn more about you without much effort. A well-produced explainer video can take the place of your sales team and free up their time to engage with high quality prospects. It alleviates the need for your sales people to give the same pitch over and over.

Videos can communicate complex business ideas through animated motion graphics. They're great for explaining data and statistics, and often are paired with animated characters or elements. They're relatively inexpensive to produce and don't require on-camera presenters or setting up lighting and backgrounds.

Benefit/culture videos

What are the benefits of working with your company? This type of video explains what you do, who you do it for, and the unique benefits your organization provides. These can be animated or involve members of your company based on what style your audience prefers. Keep in mind, benefit videos are typically placed prominently on your site, such as the home page, so they should be made with the highest-quality possible.

Demo videos

These videos show how your product or service works. This video can show a complex product or service in a way that breaks it down to a simpler set of steps. Potential clients and customers want to know how to engage with your products or services, and showing them is a great way to inform them.

How-to videos

These are very popular and can be focused on both potential clients and current customers. Showing the user "how" is a great way to engage with them and to inform them without using other internal customer service resources. These videos don't have to look as professional as some of the other types mentioned here. What is important is that they are concise, focused and informational. The best way to make sure your video includes these three attributes to research your topic. Even if you're an expert, you'll want to refresh on the steps and information that will be presented in your video.

Figure #91: How-to video example

You'll also want to support the video with a good script. Writing a script will help you identify the steps you'll show in the video. The script will also help make sure you don't leave anything out. Practice the steps before you shoot the video. Make sure you can easily take the steps and walk through the script on a practice run or two or three. The viewer will want to learn by watching so make sure your how-to is well-lighted and the focus is clear. Use more show and less tell during the video.

One large brand that does a great job on how-to videos is Home Depot. They produce this video type for such products as drills and saws to show them in action, and they also produce video on how-to-build projects.[69] These videos showcase the tools and products needed to complete a project. They are informative and give their customers enough information to tackle a project on their own.

---

69 http://videos.homedepot.com/detail/videos/diy-projects/video/5815638468001/how-to-build-a-doghouse?

Whiteboard videos

This form of video can be highly engaging and very educational. Explaining graphics and text on a whiteboard causes the viewer to stay more engaged and thus able to retain more of the information you are presenting. One of the most popular series of whiteboard videos was produced by Rand Fishkin, former CEO of Moz. This weekly video features great information on SEO and digital marketing. They are easy to produce, promote brand recognition and can grow your audience.

Figure #92: Moz's Whiteboard Friday

FAQ videos

These are arguably the easiest type of video to produce. Simply ask your sales team and your customer service team what questions they hear all the time. Then, make a video answering those questions. There are great benefits to producing this type of video, as it takes the burden off the two teams explaining the same things over and over again. It also helps your audience because they can get the answers they need and don't have to work around your business hours.

Social media video

These are videos that are meant to be viewed in your social media channels and are intended to create real-time engagement with your brand. They can help you build brand awareness and help you start a conversation with your audience. For social media video, shorter is better. It has to have a strong opening and immediately draw the attention of the viewer. You are competing for their short attention spans and you must hit it hard. Video is the format that has the most interaction on Facebook.

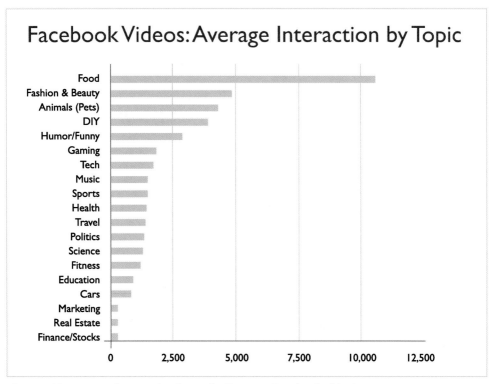

Figure #93: Average interaction by topic (Source: Facebook video)

Ad hoc videos

These are videos made on the fly. That is, creating a quick video based on a spur-of-the-moment inspiration that you want to share with your audience. Or, something that happened with you or your company where publishing a quick video can get you out ahead of everyone else. It can be a video about a new product launch where studio-quality production is not needed, or maybe a quick video on social media to show others you've arrived or are visiting at a conference. These are intended to be topical and timely based on an immediate need.

Video for your paid ads

All the types above can be repurposed for ads in social media and in display. Some may need to be adapted or edited, but for the most part, they can be easily repurposed. Remember our recommendations earlier, that every video should align with the customer journey and your business goals. If you consider the goals of each video before you produce it, it will save you time and resources since many of the videos you create will have more than one purpose and publication channel.

How can you measure the success of your videos?

We had to figure out a process to create really great content — mostly written content — about six years ago during the content marketing boom. People often told us they didn't have the resources or know-how to run their own blogs. Funny how eventually everyone adapts and figures out a way, just like we did. In order for you to reach your audience effectively, you must figure out how to produce great video (in-house) during this new video marketing boom.

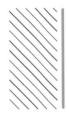

"There will be nearly 1.9 billion Internet video users by 2021."

- Cisco Visual Networking Index

You'll start slow. Maybe by using a single camera and basic editing software. But in time, your production will get smoother and higher-quality. You'll also get better at tracking any lift and determining what style you like, what works, and what doesn't, and adapt based on accurate measurement. You can determine a video's success by several criteria:

View count

Measures the raw number of views of each video or the reach of your video. Pay close attention to these metrics. Views are counted differently on the various platforms; for example, YouTube considers it a view after 30 seconds, while Facebook counts it after only 3 seconds.

Play rate

This measures how many visitors actually clicked on your video. It lets you know how relevant the video is within the context of the page it's placed on. Does it add value to the text and entice the visitor to click? Play rate is a good metric to consider for an explainer video on your home page.

Video consumption and engagement

Video consumption is about measuring the percentage of the video the user actually watched. Did they watch the whole video and then click? Did they only watch part of the video? If so, how much? You can use this data to retarget and determine the value of each video. The length of time viewers watched the video is an important factor that can give you insights as to what workflow to place them in and what ad content you will show them in your retargeting campaigns.

This is the same as measuring engagement of your blog posts and other content formats. How engaged is your audience with the content itself, the formats and publication channel? You may discover that a text post with the same information as a video is less engaging. You'll also learn which videos are the most engaging and which lead to the next click on your site.

Remember, it's not always the content that drives consumption percentage. It could be something as simple as the length of your video. Our graph measures the average drop off rate. They break the video down into three parts: the nose, the body and the tail. By looking at drop off in these three segments, they get better insights to the quality of the video and the viewer's experience. Using these insights can help you make your next video even better.

Engagement Loss by Video Length

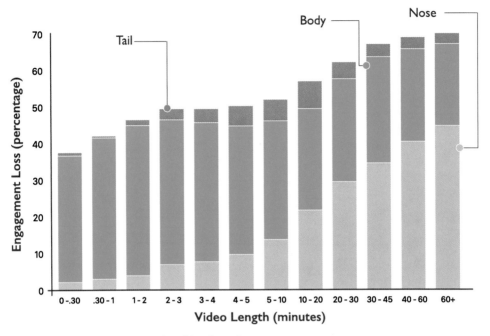

Figure #94: Engagement loss by video length

Shares, comments and conversions

How many times does your video get shared across social media channels? Social shares have the potential to grow your reach exponentially, and act as a ripple effect to reach a very large audience. As you dive into these metrics, don't just focus on the number of shares, also look at the comments and whether the viewers are leaving positive or negative comments. How many leads/customers can you attribute to a video? How many leads or sales come from an "assist" of a video view? The conversion can be anything you want it to be, like a form fill, a subscription or a purchase. The type of conversion depends on your specific customer journey and call-to-action in the video.

Assigning attribution from these channels to a specific video can be tricky. Make sure your attribution model is set up properly, and make decisions such as:

A. Only count if the video is the last content consumed before conversion (last interaction) or,
B. Only assign a certain percentage of attribution with the other content and channels that assisted a conversion.

Creating storyboards and templates

Creating storyboards will save time and help organize your thoughts and goals with each video. We highly recommend taking the time to brainstorm the content of the video and storyboard the specific shots and dialogue. This will save you from taking numerous shots and causing you to go back and reshoot scenes that you left out.

This is a great exercise if you're working with a client. You can get their input and have them involved from the very start on the direction that the video will take. Their buy-in and input will save you from reshooting a video that misses the mark for them. It will also help you produce better video as your client is closest to their customer and can give you valuable insights for better ideation.

Figure #95: Creating a video storyboard

Search for "video storyboard templates" and you'll find a variety of styles and formats. Find one that fits your level of necessary detail and test it out. You'll find many of the free templates are more than adequate for your needs. The key is to use and test it, as you'll find out what you need to change or adapt and what you can use directly from the template.

Using b-roll footage to flesh out future content

Invest time in shooting b-roll footage. It can be used over and over again to supplement other video and adds value and variation to your video shoot. Use b-roll to transition between shots and keep the action moving to make your video much more engaging. The video is intercut with the main shot and is used to help tell the story with supplemental non-talking-head video, animation, even photographs and graphics.

Make a list of the b-roll you want to create and then set up the video shoot. Making a list will give you better video and help you identify the shots you want to capture. Use your storyboard template to get just the right shots for your b-roll library. You can also buy b-roll footage, just like stock photography, with a number of websites offering free footage.[70]

Adding music to your videos

Adding music can make or break a video. It helps set the mood and helps to draw the audience into your video. Be careful in using music; much of it is copyrighted, and you'll either need permission or have to pay a royalty for the use. There are many royalty-free sources to use, so always double-check before publishing. One of the most common uses of music in video marketing is adding it to the intro or outro of your video, but finding something consistent and subtle throughout the video fills any gaps between talking points.

---

70 https://veed.me/blog/14-fantastically-free-sources-for-stock-video-footage/

Finding the right talent

You can have all the best equipment and lighting, but if the person isn't right for the camera, it drastically impacts the experience of the video (and your brand). Just like you've found good in-house writers, you'll need to find good in-house presenters that are comfortable on camera.

The video quality won't translate if the elements on screen don't engage with the audience. The same rule applies for you with written content right now: If the writing sucks, users won't read the article, and will think your website is stupid. The challenge for marketing teams this time will be that you can't find/hire good presenters as easily as you can find/hire freelance writers. The thing is, most organizations have great presenters in their office, they just haven't tried it yet.

Which video-platform is best?

There are a number of great video-processing software programs available, from straightforward editing with iMovie to sophisticated software like Adobe Premiere Pro. The sophistication of your video will dictate the functionality and features of your software.

From there, it can be hosted on several platforms:

YouTube

- 2nd largest search audience next to Google
- Don't always get positive comments or feedback
- Cannot replace a video with a new version and maintain analytics
- Ads everywhere
- Can schedule release times, unlisted & private options

Vimeo

Vimeo Basic is free. But its Paid Tier include:

- Advanced stats including plays, finishes, and comments
- Dashboard
- No ads
- Password-protected option
- Customized video player

Wistia

- Heatmaps and graphs
- Replace videos
- Force HD
- Customized video player
- Chapter videos with embed links

YouTube	Vimeo	Wistia
Cost: Free/Tiered Pricing	Cost: Free/Tiered Pricing	Cost: Free/Tiered Pricing
Features	**Features**	**Features**
• 2nd largest search audience next to Google • Don't always get positive comments or feedback • Cannot replace a video with a new version and maintain analytics • Ads everywhere • Can schedule release times, unlisted & private options	• Advanced stats including plays, finishes, and comments • Dashboard • No ads • Password-protected option • Customized video player	• Heatmaps and graphs • Replace videos • Force HD • Customized video player • Chapter videos with embed links

Figure #96: Video platform comparisons

Should you go in-house
or outsource video production?

Creating video takes time and resources, especially for businesses just getting started. Yes, the learning curve is steep. But, just like so many other organizations overcame their doubts and started creating written online content for revenue, video production will eventually become less daunting in the eyes of weary marketers everywhere. The process of script writing and storyboarding will become second nature, sometimes even skipped, because the routine of creating video will become ingrained with your digital marketing mindset and approach.

If you're going to create ongoing videos, the upfront costs associated with this can easily be justified. If you're only interested in a limited number of explainer and product videos, outsourcing might make more sense. Determine your ongoing video needs and then create a balance sheet to help make the best financial decision. If you decide to hire an agency, pay attention and watch how they set up shots closely. It's a great learning experience that can help you understand the video production process much more clearly.

Don't forget your call-to-action

One of the last and most important elements of video, of course, is the call-to-action. The same rules apply to what we covered earlier in the book – don't leave your audience hanging. Tell them what you want them to do. Embed a link that directs the user to a specific landing page on your website. This page is the logical next step in the journey for the potential customer because it provides more related information to their initial search. You can include your phone number and add any call-to-action information either during or at the end of the video. Not putting a call-to-action in your video is like making a sales pitch and not asking for the sale. Your visitor demonstrated clear interest by watching the entire video, so make the "ask" to increase your conversion rates.

The call-to-action could be to close the deal but, as mentioned above, it could be to direct the user to the next stage of the journey. For example, you could start with an explainer video and the call-to-action could lead to a video of your most recent webinar, then to a product video and then on to a testimonial. Created a detailed road map for that journey while creating more video content.

Main Takeaways
& Action Steps

1

What is your current approach to customer advocacy?
What can you improve or change?

2

What types of videos would be the most beneficial for
your customers and brand?

3

What resources do you have available to start making
videos today, and which ones might you need?

CHAPTER XIII
Re-engaging your customers for retention, repeat sales and advocacy

Coronado knows that keeping in touch with new students is important to its continued recruiting efforts, and this email workflow has proven to get great testimonials from new students. What are you doing with your current customers? Are you encouraging them to advocate for you and your products and services? If not, why?

Using nothing but her smartphone, Sophia records her own testimonial video for Coronado University. She talks about how much she enjoys the faculty, coursework and online experience. She knows the hard work will pay off in the long run, and encourages others to consider her path.

Similar to how her journey began with the Onward & Upward Talk Radio spot and content from LinkedIn a year ago, she posts her video to inspire other marketing professionals looking to advance their careers. In addition to posting the video through her social networks, Sophia heads to various review sites and give Coronado University high ratings.

Just as testimonials can reinforce your brand, reviews can have an immediate positive or negative impact on your business. If you're in the food-service space, you know how much impact reviews can have.

> **"84% of people trust online reviews as much as a recommendation from a friend or family member."**
>
> – BrightLocal

How to get more reviews on Google

According to BrightLocal, if your business has positive online reviews, users are less likely to visit your website.

Huh?

Well, if you think about it, it kind of makes sense, right? People put so much stock in how well your organization is rated on Google, Yelp and Facebook, that if they notice a 4.6-star rating (out of 5), they think, "Good is enough for me. I'll _____."

1. Call this business right now
2. Go visit the nearest store location
3. Buy this product online

Whether you're a national organization with a presence in many states or a local business, online reviews are a major factor in your prospects' buying decisions — and sometimes, they're the only factor. Marked up correctly, your star rating can display as a trust signal right in the SERPs.

We've also started to see how the digital footprint of your reviews is starting to blend with real-world recommendations from your network. Eighty-five percent of consumers trust online reviews as much as recommendations from friends and family, according to a BrightLocal study.[71]

Actively promote that you're seeking Google reviews

All things being equal, most searchers and consumers are looking for at least a 4.0-star score before they'll consider a business. If you're below this threshold, you have some work to do. Here are a few ideas to raise your score and your overall number of reviews.

Whether it's through office signage, handouts, text messages, email campaigns or the header of your website, give your audience ample opportunities, links and reminders that you have a presence on Google and that their review means a lot to you.

---

71 https://www.brightlocal.com/learn/local-consumer-review-survey/

You can make the process of writing a Google review more seamless for your customers by setting up a Google Review "quick link." To learn how, visit vert.ms/google-review-setup and follow the instructions.

Once you complete the three- to five-step process (which should take 3 minutes or less), you'll have a unique link for your business that, when entered into a browser or clicked on from an email, will display a pop-up window allowing users to immediately start writing their Google review of your company. Pretty handy, huh?

Some other things to consider:

1. That obsolete Google Plus icon you have in the footer of your website, next to your Facebook and LinkedIn icons? Replace it with a Google icon that goes straight to your new Google Review quick link.

2. Reach out to folks who have written positive reviews about you on Yelp, Amazon, TripAdvisor or Facebook, and ask them to post a similar review on Google — wait, you can do that? Yes!

Ask your customers to write reviews

It's been a misnomer for many years that businesses cannot ask their clients to write reviews (we're looking at you, Yelp). Not true — asking does not violate Yelp's terms of service (TOS).[72] What does violate their TOS is offering to compensate people in any way for writing a review about you. Don't do that!

According to Search Engine Land, 71 percent of customers will leave you a review when asked.[73] Earning more online reviews can be critical for your business, so don't be shy about this. Communicating with your customers directly (in person) or indirectly (via a 1:1 email from your CEO or a customer service rep) can drastically increase your chances of earning more reviews online.

"Among the 200+ ranking factors in Google's algorithm, about 13% of the total weight comes from online reviews."

- Search Engine Land

72 https://searchengineland.com/3-inconsistencies-yelps-review-solicitation-crackdown-288404
73 https://searchengineland.com/70-consumers-will-leave-review-business-asked-262802

Pay attention to negative reviews

Use negative reviews as teaching moments for your employees. Audit all your online reviews – especially those in Google – and see what themes, if any, exist. Share results and findings with your teams.

If you start to address common complaints from your reviews (i.e. you poorly set expectations for your product, there were hidden fees, or the wait time was excessive), you will likely improve future reviews of your business.

Research shows that by not just listening to negative reviews, but by actually responding to them consistently, you can increase your star rating.[74] Again, the more you interact with your customers – in this case, responding to their reviews – the more you show that your brand cares and wants to make it right. This habit will ultimately encourage more reviews from future customers.

Google reviews impact
your search performance

Among the more than 200 ranking factors in Google's search engine algorithm, about 13 percent of the total weight comes from online reviews. So, while you may have a 5-star rating on Facebook, if you're at 3.5 in Google, that's going to hurt your chances to perform well in the SERP. This is because Google, as part of its algorithm, only considers reviews written on its own platform.

In addition to signaling that you're a trusted brand, positive reviews can also help you get listed in Google's coveted local 3-pack, which is influenced by:

- Proximity of the searcher to your business listing's address
- Your business' overall rating (out of 5 stars)
- Quantity of reviews
- Frequency of reviews

74 https://www.inc.com/peter-roesler/new-research-reveals-secret-to-better-online-reviews.html

Online reviews are a major factor in your customers' buying decisions — and sometimes, it's the only factor. And because Google is the most common starting point for people when they begin their online research for a product or service, Google reviews may be one of the very first things that your prospects use to judge your organization. Be sure to leave them with a good impression.

Obtaining reviews is like asking for testimonials:

- Ask for the review and promote the link to your review-site business page.
- Include example reviews in your ask email to give the new customer some ideas on what to include.
- Create a video of how to do a review for your business.
- Integrate in your email workflows and track your conversions

When you're asking for reviews, include some questions to help your customers craft their reviews. This can also help them to respond by using some of your priority-keyword phrases.

For example:

- Which products or services did you buy from us?
- What location did you visit for your purchase?
- What do you like best about the product or service?
- Why do you like working with us?
- What made you choose us over the competition?
- Do you have any suggestions for others considering our products or services?

Don't sweat too much over a few bad reviews. Most reasonable prospects understand that you can't please everyone. A mix of reviews shows a normal business that pleases most, but sometimes falls short. A review can indicate that your team is strong and providing awesome service. However, it could also be the canary in the coal mine, indicating that your customer service or product quality is dropping.

The key to overcoming a bad review is a quick response that lets the reviewer know you're listening to their concerns, you've taken corrective action, and if appropriate, offers an apology. Your existing customers are more valuable than your prospects, and long-term customers even more. We all know the common mantra in business: It's a lot less expensive to keep a customer than to acquire a new one. So, how do you keep customers long-term? Using a service like Net Promoter Score can you help you gain insights as to what you're doing well as a company and areas where you need to improve. You can continue to innovate as a company and provide new products and services that support your customer's original purchase. The simplest way is to stay connected with them. It's an easy thing to do, but it's often overlooked. You have their contact information – it's up to you to keep reaching out to remind them they made the right choice in selecting you.

But how can you continue that personal relationship you worked so hard to obtain thus far? Your customer might have already converted, bought your product, started your service. How do you keep hundreds, if not thousands, of customers coming back?

Advocacy is often the most neglected part of the customer journey but can be one of the most lucrative in terms of increasing the lifetime value of a customer and for growing your audience. At this point, the prospect has already converted and become a paying customer. You have all the information you need to put them into a new workflow to re-engage with them and nurture your relationship. You know who they are, what pages they consumed on your site and what products or services they've purchased. Use these data points to create workflows with these specific outcomes in mind.

Repeat purchases: after-purchase emails

In the early 2000s, Domino's Pizza was failing. The company decided to not only improve their recipes and products (very important), they also focused on utilizing the Internet to grow their business. Because of this, they've built their owned customer database to more than 15 million customers.[75] They launched the "pizza turnaround" all the way back in 2010, but they had a tough road ahead of them.

---

75 https://money.cnn.com/2018/03/06/news/companies/dominos-pizza-hut-papa-johns/index.html

CEO Patrick Doyle, who stepped down in June, 2018, appeared in ads with Domino's workers reading blunt reviews: "worst pizza I've ever had," "sauce tastes like ketchup" and "the crust tastes like cardboard."[76]

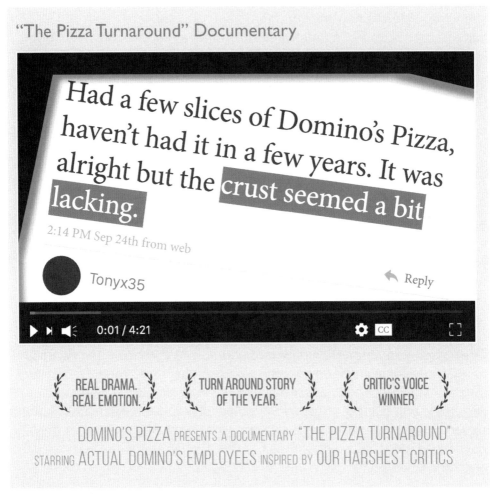

Figure #97: "The Pizza Turnaround" documentary

They took their business from $3 per share back to $258.39 per share (as of October 2018) by improving their recipes and focusing on smooth customer service in digital channels. The focus on the Internet has allowed them to develop a significant owned audience. What if you had 15 million people you could communicate with whenever you wanted? As we covered earlier, this is a significant business asset and can differentiate you from the competition.

This owned audience can be tapped whenever the company wants to add incremental sales after purchase. Domino's discovered it was much more profitable to craft well-targeted emails that targeted repeat customers than it was to focus primarily on new customer acquisition.

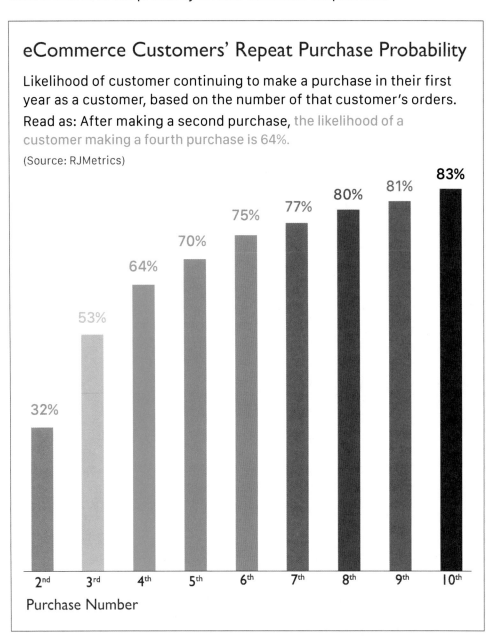

Figure #98: E-commerce customers' repeat purchase probability

According to a study by RJMetrics, there's a 32 percent chance your new customers will buy from you again.[77] The question to ask yourself is, 'Do I have any other marketing channel that converts at 32 percent?' Email marketing is the best tool for customer retention and for soliciting repeat purchases. Post-purchase emails should be segmented by the previous purchase, buying cycles and the amount of engagement customers have shown in previous emails. An engaged customer is more likely to buy again, and they can be targeted with purchase-focused messages. Don't be bashful about sending out transactional emails, they can be extremely profitable. In fact, 64 percent of consumers actually consider these the most valuable emails in their inbox, and they typically have 8 times higher open and click-through rates than promotional emails.[78]

Optimizing messaging
for ancillary purchases

You already know what your customer recently purchased. What ancillary or complimentary products or services could they use?

Send out the appropriate messaging based on what you know about the customer. Inviting them back to your online store to purchase a supporting item shows you've been paying attention. Rather than annoying them, you're providing value and giving them ideas on their next purchase.

These emails are transactional in their focus and can be segmented a number of ways:

- Last purchase and the timing: week, month, quarter, year and the repeat sales cycle
- Value of the customer (average order value)
- Category of their purchase

77 https://rjmetrics.com/resources/reports/ecommerce-buyer-behavior
78 https://rjmetrics.com/resources/reports/2015-ecommerce-growth-benchmark/

Sophia applies
for a top-level position

Shortly after graduation, Sophia left Stonecreek Digital for a Marketing Director position at a company in Carlsbad. As a proud alum, she still sports her Coronado University sweaters on casual Fridays, most often accompanied with a sense of pride and accomplishment only new graduates get the opportunity to feel. She has her own small office that faces the water: the one with lights still on late at night; the one filled with a consistent hum of energy; the one that will soon be empty.

"Thanks so much! I'm excited to meet with your team and see if we're a good fit. Talk to you soon. Take care." Sophia gently hangs up her phone and gathers her excitement. She's already prepared to move on from her new company, applying for the VP of Marketing position with an agency in downtown San Diego. It's a promotion she believes can quickly boost her career — after all, her ultimate goal is to become CMO of a large brand.

A few days after Sophia's interview, the CEO calls her with a tough break. She didn't get the job this time. Instead, it ironically went to the person who read this book. Their knowledge around the customer journey and how to build an owned audience for the agency was something the CEO couldn't possibly turn down. We swear!

In our next and final chapter, we draw this journey to a close. Read on for a recap of our top tips and techniques to help you improve your overall digital marketing and master the customer journey.

Main Takeaways
& Action Steps

1

What strategies do you currently use to encourage repeat purchases?

2

What new strategies can you consider to foster more loyalty and incremental revenue?

3

What's the one single idea from the book so far that you're excited to pursue further?

CHAPTER XIV
Tying it all together

You've seen the complete customer journey through Sophia's efforts to find the right university to further her education and enhance her career. The steps she followed to her final decision were not by accident. Rather, they were based on a well-orchestrated strategy of content marketing, paid advertising and SEO. All these resources were deployed and designed to answer her questions, provide information and be there for her in every step of the customer journey.

Sophia started her process with a problem — she wasn't feeling fulfilled in her professional life. She took the same steps any of us would take when trying to find a solution to a challenge, starting with Google search and ending with calling on the brand of choice. In walking through this process with Sophia, we learned that it's critical for brands to show up for potential customers in every facet of their customer journey using all of the tools and tactics we discussed in the previous chapters. If Magellan University hadn't engaged in traditional advertising by partnering with the radio station or had a midday time slot that wasn't during Sophia's commute, she might not have started her journey in the first place. This brand planted a seed in Sophia's mind. She might not have even thought that she was ready for a change at work until she heard that radio spot. Awareness stage content is often the hardest content to create, as individuals likely haven't identified that a problem exists in their life. Having a partnership with traditional advertising is a great way to get in front of that audience.

Had Magellan University not had a highly authoritative presence online and optimized their content for search, their content might not have shown up when Sophia first posed a question to Google. Magellan University had all the tools to nurture her through the journey. But due to a gap in their content, Sophia bounced and found what she was looking for elsewhere. Once she was ready to re-engage, after being reminded at work of why she was looking into the career move in the first place, Magellan University was nowhere to be found; however, their competitor, Coronado University, was right there, waiting like a soaking-wet Ryan Gosling after building you a house, ready to help start the next chapter of her life.

Because of Coronado's fully implemented and documented digital marketing strategy, the university was there at every stage.

They used strategies like the Hub & Spoke model, allowing them to nurture Sophia as a lead through email automation, tailored by her interests and current stage of her journey. They provided relevant and useful content to her that educated her and kept the brand top of mind. While Sophia's process took many months from start to finish, Coronado University was there for her every step of the way. Providing this consistent value to potential customers pays off in the long run when they become actual customers and, eventually, brand advocates. When you create relevant content for your audience on a consistent basis, potential customers will find that content through search or social, engage on your site and turn into business for your company.

When you step back and look at all the strategies and best practices described in this book, developing a digital marketing strategy that plans for all of it might seem daunting. And to be honest, it is — if you aren't organized. But hey, at the end of the day, creating engaging content around the industry you're passionate about is fun! You have the opportunity to demonstrate that you have expert industry knowledge, and that's not only something to be proud of, it's something to have a good time exploring. Publishing this book was an opportunity to excite our audience. It opened an avenue to put some of our online content in a book, and educate our audience on how they can succeed by strategizing around a customer journey. From this standpoint, you could say that this book accomplishes what it promotes. On the other hand, you could just say that we have a full digital marketing mindset!

How much should you budget for digital marketing this year?

After coming this far in the book, you're most likely wondering, what is all of this going to cost? The following is a recap of the most important aspects we've covered. You'll see things we've already covered, and we've included them here because of their overall importance to your success. We don't want you to leave anything out of your budget that would limit your strategy's success.

Putting together a digital strategy that includes content marketing, search optimization and promotion can be a daunting task. To some, it might seem like putting together a 1,000-piece puzzle with pieces from five different boxes and five different scenes.

For this reason, we want to offer ideas on how to plan your digital marketing budget, where to focus, tools to use, and how to allocate your budget across the different tactics.

These major elements include:

- A documented digital marketing strategy
- Research, topic ideation and a content calendar
- Keyword mapping and optimization of your content
- Content development
- Content amplification, including paid promotion and distribution
- Lead nurture
- Measurement

Building your owned audience

At Vertical Measures, we first create strategies that focus on owning an audience.[79] That means you have a prospect's name, and, at a minimum, their email address. With this information, you can communicate with them on a one-to-one basis. You don't have to further promote or advertise to them through different channels — you can set up workflows and email them directly. This owned audience becomes a business asset and can be extremely valuable.

Let's go back to two examples we covered earlier in the book:

Domino's Pizza

In 2008, Domino's Pizza was struggling and its stock price had plummeted to $3 per share.[80] The following year, after some bad press and really bad-tasting pizza, Domino's started its comeback. The turnaround was all about making better pizza and focusing on the digital space. They created an easy-to-order online system that accounted for more than 60 percent of their volume and set about building their database of owned audience. This audience has since grown to more than 15 million users — that's a lot of pizza!

79 https://www.verticalmeasures.com/approach/building-your-own-audience/
80 https://money.cnn.com/2018/03/06/news/companies/dominos-pizza-hut-papa-johns/index.html

Domino's can communicate directly with this audience whenever they wish. This database of an owned audience is definitely a competitive advantage. What was the impact of these strategic changes? Well, they're back to selling great pizza to happy customers, and their stock price is now at ~$260 per share.

Dollar Shave Club

Another good example of owning your own audience is the Dollar Shave Club. Many of us have seen their viral advertisement, which has been viewed more than 22 million times (and was mentioned back in chapter 12). As you'll recall, this video resulted in more than 12,000 sales within the first 48 hours of publication.

Dollar Shave Club (DSC) is a direct-to-consumer company. They own their audience. They were able to cut out the retailer and go direct. They've built their business with monthly recurring revenue (subscription-based sales) and referrals. In fact, "50,000 people a month refer a friend to the club," said DSC founder Michael Dubin in an interview with CNBC.[81]

This is one of the reasons Unilever recently bought DSC for $1 billion. As a consumer-packaged goods (CPG) company, Unilever sells mostly wholesale through retailers. By having DSC's owned audience, they can go direct at retail pricing. So, not only can they sell razors, shaving cream and the other products from DSC, they can also add in ancillary CPG products and grow their profits through monthly recurring revenue.

The customer journey: a recap

The customer journey is all the steps a prospect takes to make a purchase decision — and they do it with or without you.[82]

We use a four-stage customer journey:

1. AWARENESS
2. CONSIDERATION
3. DECISION
4. ADVOCACY

---

81 https://www.cnbc.com/video/2017/09/27/razor-sharp-a-conversation-with-michael-dubin.html
82 https://www.verticalmeasures.com/approach/the-customer-journey/

Your journey may be similar or even more complex. The idea is to understand what steps a customer will take along the way to making a purchase from your organization. Once you know the steps involved, you can audit your website to make sure you have content in each stage of their journey. We often find our customers have a lot of content in the decision stage, but are lacking in the other three.

How the customer journey impacts sales

OLD   NEW

Marketing ———— AWARENESS

                                                       Marketing

                  CONSIDERATION

Sales   DECISION ———————— Sales

                  ADVOCACY ———————— Marketing

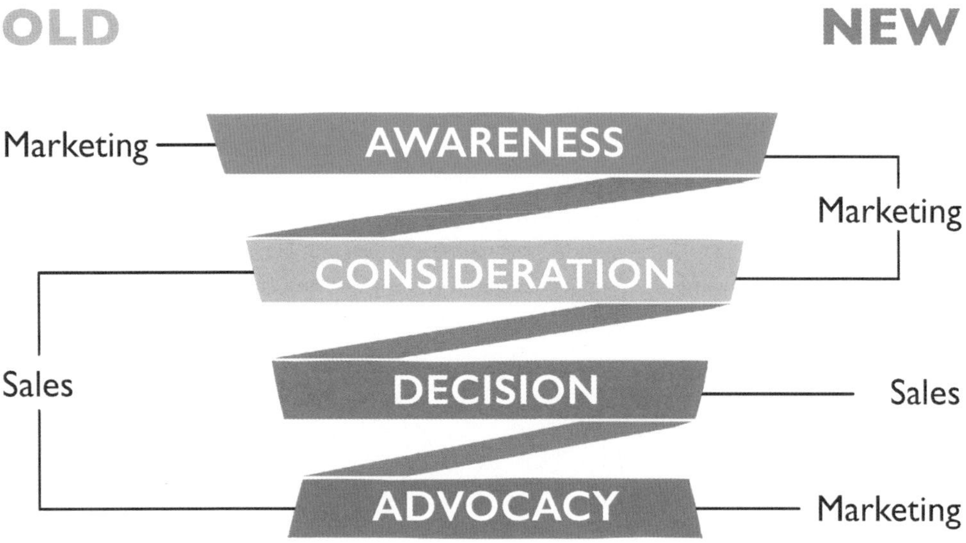

Figure #99: How the customer journey impacts sales

How much content do you need in each stage?

In the customer journey, awareness is your biggest opportunity. You want a lot of awareness content, so consider creating 50 percent of your content to target the awareness stage of your personas' journeys, 30 percent for consideration, 15 percent for decision and 5 percent for advocacy. These recommendations make a great starting point, but you should base your content mix on your specific industry, audience and sales cycle. Use our figures as a benchmark if you have no idea where to start. A content gap analysis can help you determine how much content you have for each stage compared to your target percentages.

Content & The Customer Journey

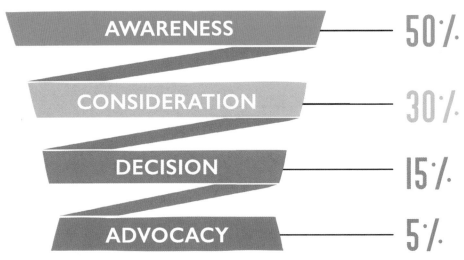

Figure #100: Creating enough content for each stage

Content has the power to move users to the decision stage without any sales intervention. That's a good thing because most of us are sales avoiders. Marketing, including digital marketing, is responsible for more of the customer journey today — sales doesn't really get involved until the decision stage.

Content marketing
is maturing

At the beginning of the book, we mentioned that our team travels around the world hosting marketing workshops. When we started presenting these workshops, most of our audience wasn't familiar with the concept of content marketing or its role in digital marketing. Now, almost the entire audience is familiar with the concept and already participating in digital content marketing to some degree.

How would you describe your organization's content marketing maturity level?

SOPHISTICATED	MATURE	ADOLESCENT	YOUNG	BABY STEPS
7%	**29%**	**28%**	**26%**	**10%**
Providing accurate measurement to the business, scaling across the organization	Finding success, yet challenges with integration across the organization	Have developed a business case, seeing early success, becoming more sophiscated with measurement and scaling	Growing pains, challenges with creating a cohesive strategy and a measurement plan	Doing some aspects of content, but have not yet begun to make content marketing a process

Figure #101: B2C organizations' content marketing maturity level
(Source: Content Marketing Institute 2018 B2C Trends Report)

In fact, according to the most recent B2C trends report from Content Marketing Institute, 86 percent of organizations say they are using digital content marketing. Now, the biggest concern is how to get those content marketing efforts to produce consistent results.

First, you want to ensure your marketing strategy is actually working. You'd be surprised, but some companies are still unclear about what digital marketing really involves. They get it confused with branded advertising. Your digital content should be answering questions, solving problems and reaching your audience at every stage of the sales funnel. If you're just talking about yourself, you're doing it wrong.

> **Content marketing is like a first date.**
>
> **if all you do is talk about yourself, there won't be a second date.**

- David Beebe,
VP of Global Creative and Content Marketing, Marriott International

Getting Started

To create content that reaches your target audience wherever they are and moves them along the customer journey, you'll likely need to increase or at least redistribute your budget.

- How much of your overall marketing budget are you spending on digital marketing?
- Will you spend more or less on digital marketing in the coming year?
- Is your digital marketing program effective? How do you know?
- Where can you get the additional funds you need to increase the frequency of publication or grow your channel distribution?
- What will you measure to determine if your program is successful?

You'll need to consider content, promotion and measurement for each stage of the journey and how they relate to one another. You'll need to look beyond just the content, at how you'll promote it and measure the KPIs that are most important to your success.

How much should new and established companies spend?

The answer to this question is simple: It depends. We know that's not very helpful when setting your budget for digital marketing. So, first, you need to answer a few other questions. Are you in a mature industry, a new niche or a very competitive category? Determining that will help you start to establish an appropriate budget.

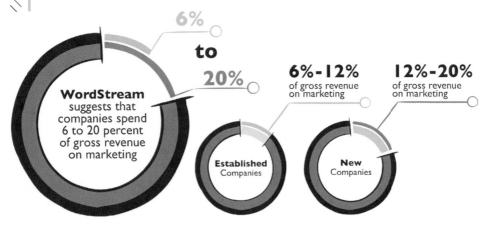

Figure #103: Suggested marketing budgets as percentage of total budget (Source: WordStream)

Established brands can spend less than startups, as they should already have loyal returning customers. A new company, or one that is in a very competitive space, needs to allocate more. If you're a CPG company, you'll be at the top of the budget-spend list. Although there's no definitive percent of your gross revenue that you should spend, these benchmarks should at least give you a few ideas on where to start.

There are a few areas to focus on as you plan your digital marketing budget. To get your content found and consumed, it really boils down to allocating budget for these four things:

- Creating content that resonates with your audience
- Optimizing the content for high search visibility
- Promoting the content to drive your audience to your site
- Distributing the content to drive new audience discovery

There are three ways to accomplish these four tasks: You can...

do it all
yourself

hand
everything
over to the
experts or...

collaborate
with an
agency

Each approach has its own advantages and disadvantages along with different degrees of expense. While turning all your content marketing over to an agency could be the most costly approach, it could also be the fastest to implement and, in turn, see ROI.

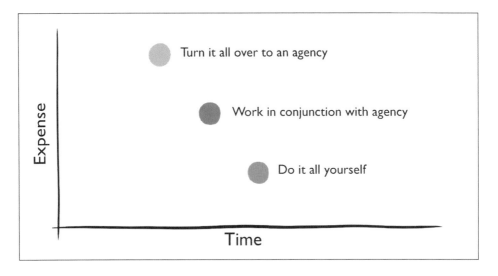

Doing it all yourself can be the least expensive, but it will take the longest to implement. You'll also be limited based on how much expertise you have directly related to digital marketing and the resources you have available.

The third way to deploy a digital marketing strategy is to do it in conjunction with an agency. Piggyback on their expertise and resources, while learning and implementing best practices across your organization. We think this third way is the sweet spot because no one knows your business better than you do, but an agency can strategically turn your expertise into targeted, deep, strategic content.

Is there a correlation
between marketing budget and effectiveness?

In a recent survey by Content Marketing Institute, the average B2C organization spends 26 percent of its overall marketing budget on content marketing. The report also found a correlation between the most effective programs and the percent of spend.

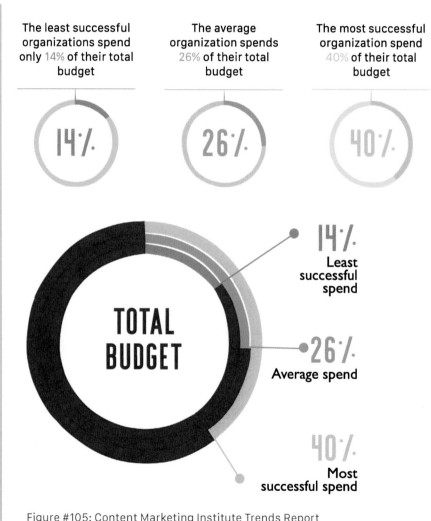

The least successful organizations spend only 14% of their total budget

The average organization spends 26% of their total budget

The most successful organization spend 40% of their total budget

14%
Least successful spend

TOTAL BUDGET

26%
Average spend

40%
Most successful spend

Figure #105: Content Marketing Institute Trends Report
(Source: CMI 2018 B2C Trends Report)

B2C marketers that allocated 40 percent of their budget to content marketing were the most effective, while marketers that spent 14 percent were the least effective. Of those companies surveyed, 37 percent said they expect their content marketing budgets to increase in the next year.

How to find hidden funds
for digital marketing

There are two ways to find funds for your digital marketing budget. One way is to just add dollars as newly available funds. The other, more practical way is to take funds from marketing strategies that are no longer effective. For example, many companies are taking dollars away from their traditional advertising and moving them to digital marketing.

Now that you have an idea of where you are going to allocate your budget, you'll need to determine the overall budget needed and, in some cases, where you're going to find the investment dollars. But first, decide on how deep you want to go. There are three levels of involvement and commitment in digital marketing. Where do you see yourself?

1. We're novices and are just getting our feet wet.
2. We know it's important but not everyone is on board yet.
3. We're all-in and on our way to creating a culture of content marketing.

Asking for a **small percentage** of a **larger advertsing budget** for short-lived campaigns is a good place to start looking for budget donations.

— NewsCred

In a great slide deck they've posted on SlideShare, NewsCred suggests that you start looking to fund your marketing budget by advocating for a small piece of a larger, already established budget — like an advertising budget.[83]

Because content marketing allows you to **gain additional reach**, engagement and conversion without having to pay for it, you can literally **earn your audience's attention** versus buying it.

— Liz Bedor, NewsCred
(for Marketing Insider Group)

83 https://www.slideshare.net/NewsCred/how-to-calculate-content-marketing-roi-51315907/32-Asking_for_a_small_percentage

How can you justify
your digital marketing budget?

Visitors who find your website through a branded search likely already know about you and your organization's offerings. Since they've done a direct search for your name, we can assume they either already know and trust your brand, or they're in the consideration or decision stage of their conversion process, and you're in the running for their business. On the other hand, someone that gets to your site through an unbranded organic search didn't really know where they would end up when typing in their search query. Because your website showed up in the search results, your content marketing efforts have been proven to work and attract top-of-the-funnel, awareness stage prospects.

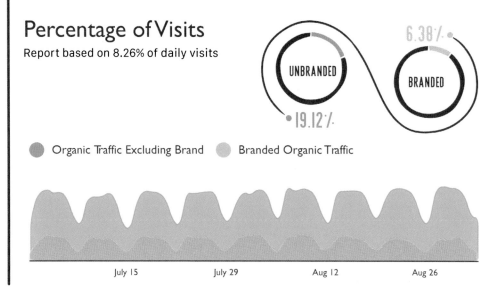

Figure #108: Unbranded vs. branded search (Source: Google Analytics)

It's important to capture these non-branded organic metrics as they will help you justify and potentially expand your digital marketing budget. Remember, once your content starts resonating with search engines, this traffic will continue. Include paid advertising and you can dominate search completely.

The fact is, you can gain new customers by providing useful, helpful, entertaining or relevant content consistently. Someone who may never have found your site can be nurtured over time, drawn through your customer journey and, ultimately, led to a conversion.

> Investing your resources (i.e. time and money) into content marketing will reduce your cost, while simultaneously generating up to 3x the leads you'd have gotten with native or traditional advertising.
>
> — Neil Patel, entrepreneur, investor, influencer and co-founder of Neil Patel Digital

What's a good ROI for digital marketing?

A 5:1 ratio is considered middle-of-the-road in terms of ROI. A 10:1 ROI on digital marketing is awesome. Keep in mind, however, your ratio will be dependent on the length of your sales cycle and your ability to establish and track conversions. It will also depend on the competitive nature of your industry. By knowing these data points and doing the math, you can calculate what a new customer is worth and how much you are willing to spend in order to acquire that new customer.

Use our digital calculator to help you develop your digital marketing budget and better understand the cost/benefit analysis of your digital marketing:

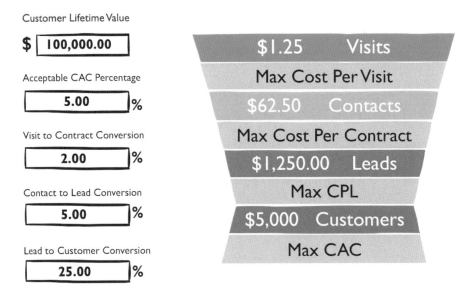

Customer Lifetime Value
$ 100,000.00

Acceptable CAC Percentage
5.00 %

Visit to Contract Conversion
2.00 %

Contact to Lead Conversion
5.00 %

Lead to Customer Conversion
25.00 %

$1.25 Visits
Max Cost Per Visit
$62.50 Contacts
Max Cost Per Contract
$1,250.00 Leads
Max CPL
$5,000 Customers
Max CAC

Figure #110: Vertical Measures' digital marketing calculator
(www.verticalmeasures.com/resources/digital-marketing-calculator/)

Lifetime Value (LTV)

What is the lifetime value of your customer? If you sell a one-and-done product, it's really easy to determine. If you have monthly recurring revenue (MRR) and your customers stay with you for years, it's a bit more difficult to determine.

Here's a very simple formula you can use:

Lifetime Revenue (LTR)

LTR = (average purchase price) **x** (average purchase frequency)

LTV = (average gross margin) **x** (LTR)

Cost Per Visit (CPV)

How much does every visit to your site cost? In most cases, you should know both organic and paid numbers. You can also get very granular and determine the cost per visit by channel. This will help you assign attribution to the different channels and tactics you are using.

Cost Per Lead (CPL)

Determine how much it costs to have a website visitor become a lead. A lead can be defined many ways depending on your sales cycle and business products and services. A lead to you might be someone that fills out a form or someone that engages with three or more pieces of content on your site. Whatever your definition is, you should know the cost of generating that lead.

Customer Acquisition Cost (CAC)

How much does it cost you to acquire each customer? The formula is simple: Take your overall marketing expenses and divide by the number of customers. For example, if you spend $1,000 on marketing and get 10 new customers, the cost of acquisition is $100 per customer. You'll need to determine your maximum threshold for new customer cost, which you can base off of their LTV or a different metric you feel comfortable with to start. Our goal (and a goal of digital marketing) is always look for way to reduce the CAC.

Determining customer acquisition cost from digital marketing

Want to take your calculations a step further and understand your customer acquisition cost from digital marketing? It's easy to measure paid advertising results since you can drive clicks to landing pages and measure conversions. However, it's more difficult to track conversions from various digital marketing channels working together. Not impossible, just more difficult.

Can you justify your customer acquisition cost?

Devesh Khanal describes in detail how to determine the customer acquisition cost of digital marketing. His guidance provides some very solid ideas on how to track and quantify your results. Khanal also offers a downloadable customer acquisition calculator to help you organize your data.[84] If you really want to dig in, he also has a webinar that walks you through figuring out your customer acquisition cost.[85]

> [Customer acquisition cost for content marketing] depends on the value of a single customer to your company, which is most often represented in two ways:
> 1) Monthly recurring revenue of a single customer: MRR **or**
> 2) Lifetime value of a single customer: LTV

— Devesh Khanal, Co-Founder of Grow and Convert

How much is enough for your digital marketing budget?

Without getting into specific budget numbers, marketing growth strategist Derek Halpern explains what you should be thinking about as you deploy your upcoming digital marketing strategy. His recommendation is to spend only 20 percent of the time creating content and 80 percent of your time promoting and distributing your content.

---

84 https://growandconvert.com/content-marketing/customer-acquisition-cost/

85 https://www.youtube.com/watch?v=ywcJvXzfju8&feature=youtu.be&t=2m

Halpern's reasoning is that the market is oversaturated with mediocre content, so brands must create significantly better content, and then promote the heck out of it to succeed.

There are massive amounts of content being published every day. You've got to create content that stands out, and you've also got to amplify your content to be seen. Both steps are designed to increase the reach of your content and the potential audience of people that can interact with and share it. Don't miss these important steps. Make sure to include adequate budget for creation, promotion and distribution in your overall plan. Do you have a plan and the funds to effectively support all three?

20%
Creating
content

Time Spent

80%
Promoting &
distributing

How to allocate budget
for traditional vs. online marketing

Don't fall in love with the mediums you're currently using. Traditional marketing doesn't work as well as it used to. You need to be where your customers are consuming content, and that landscape is constantly shifting. In a very NSFW video on YouTube (that's also highly motivating), entrepreneur Gary Vaynerchuk suggests that you need to spend 5 to 20 percent of your time or money on new innovative things to stay competitive says — content marketing can be one of them.[86]

---

86 https://www.youtube.com/watch?v=wDAJEjWjrCc

How much should you spend on online marketing in total?

If you need some ideas on how to allocate your overall digital budget, the breakdowns below can help you get started. You'll learn how businesses have grown and allocated funds for digital marketing over the years and all the different channels to consider in your budget. If you're creating a digital marketing budget from scratch, it makes sense to see what other organizations are spending. You can use their spend to help justify the budget you'll need.

When building your budget, the length of your sales cycle and other aspects of your business might cause you to increase or decrease your budget compared to these averages, but this info will give you a good idea on where to begin.

In general, companies average an increase in spend of around $200 for email marketing year over year (YOY), while both display advertising and social media saw an average increase of around $2,000 to YOY. Search marketing is also an area that sees substantial spend increases YOY.

Email marketing

2019	2018	2017	2016	2015	2014
$3,067	$2,865	$2,665	$2,466	$2,266	$2,067

$4,000

Social media

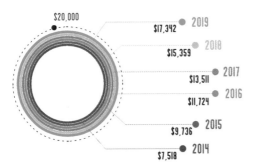

$20,000

- $17,342 — 2019
- $15,359 — 2018
- $13,511 — 2017
- $11,724 — 2016
- $9,736 — 2015
- $7,518 — 2014

Display advertising

$40,000

2019	$37,574
2018	$34,477
2017	$31,281
2016	$27,916
2015	$23,680
2014	$19,801

Search marketing

Total Spend
(in millions)

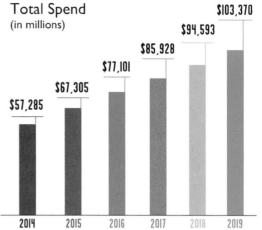

As you put together your editorial calendar and prioritize what content to create, consider all the channels and kinds of content you'll need to effectively move people through the customer journey.

Here are some reminders of the kinds of content you can publish and where they might fit in a strategic Hub & Spoke model:

- Lists
- How-to guides
- Q&A content
- Testimonials
- Case Studies
- Blog Posts
- White Papers
- Interviews
- Curated posts
- Free Guides
- Videos
- Infographics
- Templates
- Calculators
- Checklists

Who do you need
to support your digital marketing strategy?

We talk to organizations all the time that are debating whether to hire more in-house resources to handle a full digital marketing strategy or hire an agency. While it may seem like staying in-house is a cost-cutting way to take control of your own marketing efforts, the math rarely adds up.

See for yourself:

Figure #114: Estimated costs of an in-house digital marketing team

XIV: *Tying it all together* | 293

If the true cost of an in-house marketing team seems overwhelming, consider sharing the responsibilities (and expense) with an agency. **The best agency-client relationship is a true partnership.** It should be your agency's job to use their expertise and skill to advance your brand, boost your traffic and take steps for you to own your audience. They'll need to collect data, analyze that data and report back to you on what the data means and what their next steps will be. Ideally, the responsibilities are broken down like this:

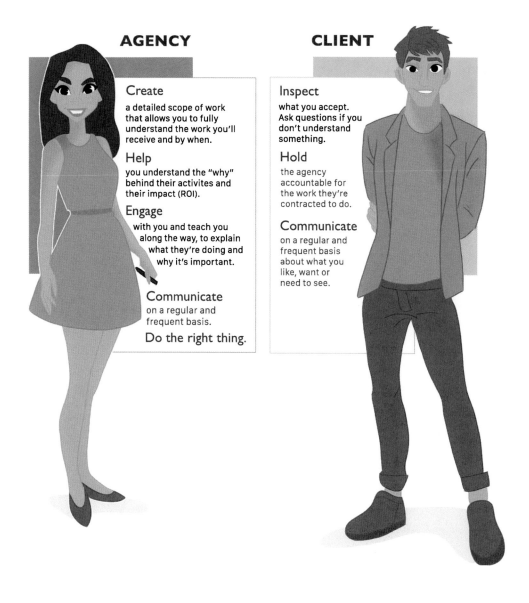

AGENCY

Create
a detailed scope of work that allows you to fully understand the work you'll receive and by when.

Help
you understand the "why" behind their activites and their impact (ROI).

Engage
with you and teach you along the way, to explain what they're doing and why it's important.

Communicate
on a regular and frequent basis.

Do the right thing.

CLIENT

Inspect
what you accept. Ask questions if you don't understand something.

Hold
the agency accountable for the work they're contracted to do.

Communicate
on a regular and frequent basis about what you like, want or need to see.

Do you feel your business is lacking in any area that was discussed in this book? Do you have business goals that can be met through digital efforts but don't have a documented digital marketing strategy to guide the way? Are you having trouble creating, designing and optimizing content that your audience is actually searching for? Are your competitors amplifying their content in a more effective way, capturing an audience you could be bringing into your funnel?

Create a strategy
and grow your owned audience

How do you get started? It all starts with having a documented strategy. Again, what we have learned over the last several years is that there is a direct correlation between having a written strategy and seeing digital marketing success — especially for companies who are just beginning to understand the need to shift your focus to digital marketing.

Take the time to create your digital marketing strategy now and the odds are you will see greater and greater success in the years to come.

Main Takeaways
& Action Steps

1

What are the first three steps you need to take to build or improve your digital marketing strategy?

2

What people or resources do you need to accomplish these first steps?

3

What new training, education or guidance do you or your people require to succeed?

Notes

Notes

Grow Your Owned Audience
with Vertical Measures

We help our clients grow their owned audience by leveraging their industry expertise and fusing it with more than 10 years of digital marketing success.

GLOSSARY

A

advocacy – When a verified customer creates content (an article, review, testimonial, video, etc.) that supports a brand.

algorithm – A group of rules set up by a search engine (i.e. Google) that sorts and ranks content.

alt text (alternative text) – Text added to an HTML document that describes an image to search engines and improves SEO.

amplify – To expand the existing reach of any given content through paid and organic promotion. Related to *Hub & Spoke*.

anchor text – The permanent, descriptive, clickable text in a link. Often appears in blue type.

AOV (average order value) – A metric that measures the average price of all orders in a certain time period.

answer box – A text box of Google-curated information that appears above search results. Often means a consumer does not have to search through other web results for the answer.

audience hierarchy – The descending value of audiences that includes *owned* (highest), *non-owned* (next valuable) and *short-term or rented* (least valuable).

awareness – When a consumer becomes aware of a topic, need, desire or goal, and connects with a web page or company about that interest for the first time.

B

b-roll footage – Additional or background footage shot to supplement the main message in a video. Can be bio information, behind-the-scenes shots, or similar content.

backlinks – Hyperlink to your page from another web page.

BANT – *Stands for budget, authority, need, and timeline*, all information that describes a potential lead.

bounce rate – The number of visitors to a website who leave after seeing only one page.

C

call-to-action – A link, button or text that uses action words to encourage a consumer to take a next step.

canonicalization – A process that insures that search engines will understand which is the preferred and/or original web page among duplicates.

conquest campaigns – When competitors purchase online ads for terms a searcher might use to find your brand or products.

consideration – The stage of a customer doing research to answer questions regarding a desire, need, or goal.

content audit – A complete evaluation of the content and its quality on a website.

content chunking – Breaking up text with lists, bullets, subheads and other devices to capture the reader's attention and keep the text from appearing dense or uninteresting.

C (continued)

CPL (cost per lead) – The average cost to an advertiser to generate a lead.

CPV (cost per view) – The price online advertisers pay for each view of their ad.

CSS3 (Cascading Style Sheets, Level 3) – Style sheets are used for formatting web pages and can control the look of text, graphics, tables and other web page components.

CTR (click-through rate) – The ratio of *users who click on a link* to the *total number of users* who receive an email or view a web page

CAC (customer acquisition cost) – How much it costs to acquire a customer through the combination of sales and marketing.

customer journey – The path through awareness, consideration, decision and advocacy that an online consumer takes.

D

decision – The choice a customer makes after considering the options.

distributed representations – Part of how queries are sorted into linguistic similarity by search engines.

E

engagement – The act of interacting with a piece of content, a website or a company.

evergreen – Content that can remain on a site for an indefinite period of time without losing its relevancy.

F

first click – A metric that credits the channel that brought a user to your website.

FOMO (Stands for "Fear of missing out") – A tactic used in advertising and social media to encourage people to take action.

friction points – Places where users tend to abandon your site.

G

gated content – Content behind a cyber wall for which something must be exchanged – either payment or personal information.

GIF – A small animated image.

GDPR – General Data Protection Regulation – A set of guidelines for European Union online privacy regulations.

H

hub – The strong center point of a content plan that generally involves a complex piece of content of high value to a consumer. Related to *spokes*.

Hub & Spoke model – A piece of primary content becomes the hub, and spokes of related content support, interact, and refer back to it.

I

ideation – The process of creating ideas for content.

impressions – The number of views a page gets, typically in advertising.

I (continued)

influencer marketing – Content generated around and by people whose position and social standing can influence others.

J

JPEG – The most common image format.

K

knowledge graph – An information fact box presented by Google next to search responses.

KPI (key performance indicators) – The most important measurable values that indicate how a company is performing.

L

landing pages – The first page a website visitor sees after clicking on a link.

last AdWords click – Used in attribution modeling, a metric that credits your AdWords campaign with a visitor.

last click – Used in attribution modeling, a metric that credits the last place your web visitor was before becoming a lead or customer.

lead-capture page – A page where visitors enter personal information to gain access or information.

LTR (lifetime revenue) – Average purchase price x average purchase frequency.

L (continued)

LTV (lifetime value) – Average gross margin x LTR.

linear attribution – A system of giving credit to multiple touchpoints that a customer encounters.

link diversity – A term that signifies the importance of having backlinks from varied websites with varied domain authority.

local 3-pack – A term for the ability to land in the top three map results for a query; 44 percent of searchers click on at least one of the three.

long-tail keywords – Searches composed of more words and phrases than old, more typical keyword searches. Often these searches provide fewer, but more relevant, results.

low-friction information – Asking a visitor for information that is simple and innocuous enough that the visitor doesn't abandon the site.

M

meta-description – An html tag that summarizes the content on a web page and is optimized for the 'click'.

metrics – Tools and measurements of consumers' interactions with the web or a website.

mobile optimization – The conscious design of web sites that allows them to work seamlessly when accessed by laptop, tablet or smartphone.

multi-touch attribution – Same as linear attribution.

N

natural search – Same as organic search.

non-gated content – Free content available to all, anonymously.

non-owned audience – A passive audience made up of visitors, podcast subscribers or social media followers who have not engaged with a website yet.

O

open rate – The ratio of *the number of people who opened an email to the total number of emails sent.*

optimizing – Using proven search engine optimization techniques to improve keyword rankings.

organic search – When a user enters a string of text into a search engine to research information.

owned audience – Someone that has traded personal information for content or through purchasing a product or service.

P

personas – Created characters that represent different audience segments of your targeted content.

PNG – A file format for image compression.

Q

R

reciprocal links – Backlinks between two independent websites.

referring domain – The domain from which a backlink originated.

retargeting – Displaying your advertising messages to users that have previously visited your site as they are visiting other websites. Also called remarketing.

root domain – The primary domain, which includes all subdomains and URLs associated with a website.

S

sales funnel – A concept based on leading consumers from awareness to research to purchase.

segmentation – Separating your email list into groups of similar recipients, typically based on demographics, geography or interests.

semantic phrases – Words and phrases spoken naturally – often through voice text on smartphones – that provide context and intent to the search engines.

search intent – A search engine understanding what the user wants even when the words used in the search are implied rather than explicit.

smarketing – A HubSpot-coined term referring to alignment between sales and marketing teams.

SQL (sales-qualified leads) – Leads that are moving from the consideration stage into the decision stage.

social capital – When a person's following is large and/or influential

S (continued)

within the space of his or her industry, meaning he or she often is retweeted, shared, and quoted.

spam score – A metric that measures how closely aligned any given site, subdomain or email is with others that have been determined to be spam.

spammy links – Obvious manipulative links that have been paid for, linking between any and all types of websites regardless of content.

spokes – Pieces of content that support and relate back to the hub piece of content. See Hub & Spoke.

strategic initiatives – Plans and tactics that will help a business achieve its business goals.

subdomain – A domain within a domain. A main domain can have nearly an unlimited number of subdomains.

T

10x content – A term coined by Rand Fishkin, it means content that is 10 times better than the content offered by the top 10 sites in a browser's search results for your keywords.

tags – Words (like keywords) that label the content in html format to help search engines identify the focus of a page.

total opens – The total number of times an email newsletter has been opened by recipients, even if some have opened it more than once. Related to *unique opens*.

touchpoints – All the stops along the path of a customer's journey in which he or she interacts with content.

U

UI (user interface) – Any means by which a user interacts with a computer system, a website or content. Related to *user experience*.

unique opens – The number of recipients that have opened an email newsletter. Each recipient is counted only once even if he or she has opened an email more than once. Related to *total opens*.

UX (user experience) – The term for whether a user finds a computer, software, or a website intuitive and pleasurable. Related to *user interface*.

V

verticals – Can have either of two meanings. Vertical content goes deeper and deeper into one specific area (as opposed to horizontal content, which would be wider and more shallow). Vertical also is the term for content designed to be easily optimized on mobile devices.

W

webinar – Coined by combining the terms "web" and "seminar," it is an informational video or whiteboard presentation that can be viewed online by a user.

whitepaper – A report about a complex topic that explores all sides of the issue to help readers understand it. Typically, it ends with the company's stance on the issue.

WIFM? – Stands for "What's in it for me?" and represents the need for a company to know as much as possible about the consumer it is targeting and what motivates that consumer to seek out content.

XYZ

INDEX

A

C

D

G

I

K

L

P

S

V